The Expert Expert
WITNESS

More Maxims and Guidelines
for Testifying in Court

Stanley L. Brodsky

American Psychological Association

Washington, DC

Published by
American Psychological Association
750 First Street, NE
Washington, DC 20002

Copies may be ordered from
APA Order Department
P.O. Box 92984
Washington, DC 20090-2984

In the U.K., Europe, Africa, and the Middle East, copies may be ordered from
American Psychological Association
3 Henrietta Street
Covent Garden, London
WC2E 8LU England

Designed and typeset in Bauer Bodoni Boldface, Garamond Light, and Dom Casual by EPS Group Inc., Easton, MD

Printer: Port City Press, Inc., Baltimore, MD
Illustrator: Margaret Scott
Cover Designer: Minker Design, Bethesda, MD
Technical/production editors: Catherine R. W. Hudson and Jennifer Powers

Library of Congress Cataloging-in-Publication Data
Brodsky, Stanley L., 1939–
    The expert expert witness : more maxims and guidelines for
testifying in court / Stanley L. Brodsky.—1st ed.
        p.   cm.
    Includes bibliographical references.
    ISBN 1-55798-597-9 (alk. paper)
    1. Evidence, Expert—United States.   2. Psychology, Forensic.
I. Title.
KF8965.B757   1999
347.73'67—dc21   99-27655
                                                               CIP

British Library Cataloguing-in-Publication Data
A CIP record is available from the British Library.

Printed in the United States of America
First Edition

Contents

Preface

I HAD GIVEN THE TITLE "The Expert Witness" for the workshop I had agreed to lead for the 1998 statewide meeting of the Florida Child Protection Teams. When I received a copy of the announcement for the workshop from Dr. Jay Whitworth, the head of the statewide organization, the flyer was titled "The Expert Expert Witness." I was surprised and delighted. The title was so appealing that I asked for and received Jay's gracious permission to use it as the title for this book, instead of my bland working title "Testifying in Court, Volume 2." Sometimes these fortuitous events shape how one thinks about a subject. Some years ago, I had agreed to give a talk to the Department of Design at Southern Illinois University on the topic of "Psychology and Law." When I arrived, the posters announced that I would be speaking on "Psychology and Law— The Space Between." I was transfixed; I tossed out my prepared remarks and launched into an excited discussion of the conceptual, scientific, and operational space between psychology and law. Still on this intellectual high after my talk, I asked my hosts how they happened to revise the title of my talk in such a meaningful and creative way. "We did not revise it at all," they explained. "We scheduled you in a new room between two geodesic domes, a room with no official room number yet, that we call 'The Space Between.'"

That's just what happened with Jay Whitworth's title. I started thinking about the book as a means toward helping expert witnesses become more expert: not more expert in their assessments or their scientific work—others have done that ably—but in their testimony. The goal is assisting readers toward becoming more expert as experts, a process one might think of as meta-expertise. Many witnesses are at the least uncomfortable and at the most seriously frightened by aggressive cross-examination during trials and aggressive questioning during depositions. This book is intended to help witnesses be wiser about the contexts in which they are asked questions and more skilled in their presentation and explanations of their findings, conclusions, and opinions.

As in the first volume, I have followed the suggestion of Norman Poythress to organize the chapters alphabetically. Readers may start anywhere, stop anywhere, without losing continuity.

The one exception to the start anywhere, stop anywhere rule is this: Start with the first volume. This book is written with the assumption that you will have been familiar with my *Testifying in Court* book. This book picks up where the earlier book leaves off. In addition to more principles, more lessons, and more maxims, there are also more instances of challenging testimony from individuals who have written or emailed me. All of the excerpts from letters, emails, testimony, and case examples in the text are presented with permission of the named individuals.

A number of books about court testimony have come out in the past few years. These books are visible and some are valuable enough that I have written an annotated bibliography of recommended books, which appears in the Appendix.

Let me close by describing my philosophy in this book. It is not a book of research or of methods for doing psychological work. What I have tried instead is to share how I understand and approach court testimony. The book is at times playful and irreverent, largely because so many experts are fearful witnesses, and humor diminishes fear. At other times the book is goal-directed at managing worst-case scenarios of being examined. Except for people who are on the witness stand regularly, testifying is a big deal, and it is my hope that these approaches will help decatastrophize what it means to be in the witness box.

If you have comments about these ideas or wish to send me descriptions of your own testifying experiences for the next volume of this book series (I promise not to title it "The Expert Expert Expert Witness"), please write to me at: Stanley L. Brodsky, Department of Psychology, The University of Alabama, Tuscaloosa, AL 35487-0348.

Acknowledgments

C HARLES PATRICK EWING, MARK MAYS, AND BRONWEN LICHTENSTEIN generously offered their reviews, their ideas, and their editorial expertise in the completion of this book. Their feedback on early drafts of the book profoundly influenced what I wrote, and I am indebted to them. Marc Boccaccini and Marla Domino helped with drafts of individual chapters, and Annette Brodsky offered helpful case information. The observant reader will note that two other Brodskys are mentioned in the book: Carroll Brodsky (my uncle) and Archie Brodsky. Despite the appearance of literary nepotism, it is just coincidence that the three Brodskys have been cited; they are unrelated to one another. Many expert witnesses have written to me and shared their experiences and observations. Their reports of testimony in trials and depositions have been included as integral parts of many chapters. I am grateful for their generous contributions.

1

Arbitrary Pigeonholes

T HE SCENES WERE AS AMUSING to watch as they were painful to endure. Attorney Frank Branson played what he called "video depositions from hell," in which hapless witnesses gave pathetic testimony in depositions. One physician-defendant offered example after example of his unethical behavior, including drinking on duty and his various suspensions of hospital privileges. An official responsible for safety in a truck fleet argued that the absence of running lights and effective brake drums did not interfere with his vehicles' perfectly safe condition. An airline official explicitly acknowledged how gross negligence by the maintenance crew had led to a fatal accident. A defendant in a civil case replied to all questions by stating, in a seeming admission of liability, that he will not answer questions, and on the advice of his lawyer he invokes his constitutional privilege against self-incrimination.

These depositions are entertaining because they are so horrifying. The errors are so serious that the obvious advice I would give the novice is to avoid being deposed in such ways. Do not say stupid things and do consider the consequences of what you say. Understand what the case is about. Check with your lawyer before answering automatically, and do not let opposing counsel take complete charge.

A more provocative lesson that emerged was Mr. Branson's use of a subtle and powerful technique of questioning. In this technique the questioner constructs seemingly sensible but arbitrary pigeonholes into which the witnesses unthinkingly place answers. The Branson form uses letter grades for the witnesses to judge their actions on the issue in dispute.

With a polite tone of voice and an open expression of interest, Branson asks the witness "How would you grade the safety conditions of these trucks? Would you give them an A? an A+? B, C? D? or an F?" The witness never hesitates. Without thinking about the issue of grades or carefully considering what the answers may mean, witnesses immediately assign a grade. This kind of questioning is a skilled trap constructed to pull witnesses into a response mode that is incompatible with their best ways of thinking about the issues. The trap is in the same family as the following questions: "Would you say you are at least 90% percent correct today?" and "On a scale of one to ten, how fully has your company met the federal guidelines?"

The sneaky part of the trap is that all of us are accustomed to the assignment of letter grades (and percentages and 10-point rating scales) throughout our educational and work experiences, and often through work and other settings. (After The University of Alabama football games, one local sports columnist assigns letter grades to the offense, defense, special teams, game plan, coaching, and incentive to win.) Letter grades and ratings are so much a part of our lives that it is rare we think twice about using them in a deposition or trial.

However, letter grades categorize the subject matter into a 5-point scale, each of which carries a potent evaluative component. You may ask, so what? The answer is that few things in life (school grades included, if you can recall your indignation at grades not being truly representative of school performance) lend themselves to a true fit into nonoverlapping labelling. Think about the last time you cleaned up after a meal; now try to assign a letter grade to the quality of that work. Think of a discussion with a new colleague; try to assign a letter grade. These are not easy or necessary tasks.

More goes on than trying to fit experiences and knowledge into rating scales; a process of unhealthy simplification occurs. I think of evaluations I have completed: some aspects were better than others; some pieces of my findings were more compelling than others. The knowledge we have about any event or problem that led to a lawsuit always has multiple components.

How should one reply to a Frank Branson question like our initial example? I suggest the following:

- "The issues do not lend themselves to simple letter grades," or
- "I would not for a second consider putting all of the hours and information I have been discussing into such an elementary way of thinking," or
- "Such simplistic speculations fall outside the nature of customary professional work and would do a disservice to the assessment," or
- "There are so many elements and issues that I would want to consider how to put them together and decide whether they allow a single letter grade to be assigned" or, finally, the related response
- "It would be misleading to assign a grade. At the very least I would have to think through how to divide this issue into its many components and then attempt to assign a grade to each component that allows for such grading."

At the conference at which we were both speaking, I told Mr. Branson how I would decline to answer a rating scale question. He indicated that he would insist that I answer the question and that if I did not, I would appear to be defensively withholding. Maybe or maybe not. Nevertheless, a broader principle applies here. When faced with such efforts by opposing counsel to condense your narrative explanations into a narrow and simplistic number or letter, you should proceed with great caution.

The Maxim: Do not allow your reports or testimony to be recast into simple-minded and arbitrary groupings of the attorney's choice.

Asked and Answered

I N AN IDEAL WORLD, expert witnesses would be able to answer attorneys' questions with full and developed explanations. Such explanations offer a context in which answers are meaningfully seated. Because the objective of adversarial questioning is the development of a single and unequivocal statement for one side or the other, cross-examination questions are often phrased in such a way to elicit endorsements of a position, or to elicit some indication of possible support for that position. Furthermore, skilled cross-examination questions are phrased in such a way as to deny the opportunity to explain, and, instead, to bring out simple, singular (as opposed to complex and explanatory) affirmations of support for the possibilities.

There are reasons to be prepared to give a singular answer; it moves the examination process along, the questioning attorney is entitled to have witnesses listen with care and then address the issue raised, and direct answers are often the only responsible reply. If the question lends itself to a *yes* or *no* answer, simple *yes* or *no* answers are appropriate and necessary. However, they are often not sufficient if they leave a substantially misleading or incorrect impression. For that reason, experienced witnesses look for chances to put the answer in an explanatory context, rather than simply to respond to a narrow and sometimes loaded question.

A difference exists between cross-examining attorneys demanding that witnesses give *yes* or *no* answers and judges making the same demand. When attorneys make this demand, witnesses are well advised to think about the question and the context in which it is seated before they give their answer. If the answer has some aspects of agreement with the attorneys' point but other aspects are not in agreement, it should be stated, preferably before actually answering the question. Consider this question, "Isn't it true, Doctor, that you don't really personally know the plaintiff, Mrs. Smith?"

The word "personally" in that question could lead witnesses to think that they do not know the plaintiff well, and a "yes" might diminish the power of the methodology, findings, and opinion. A preface to answering that question might include, "All of my professional assessments involve getting to know the individuals personally, in the ways they are as individuals. So the best way for me to answer the question is that I do not know Mrs. Smith as a friend or acquaintance, nor would I permit it in my role as a psychological evaluator, but I do indeed know a great deal about Mrs. Smith as a person."

Suppose the attorney asks, "Is it true that all of the employment and medical records you have reviewed are fallible? Please do not go into one of your long explanations and give us a simple yes or no answer."

A reasonable reply is to state, "There is no simple yes or no answer. May I explain?"

At that point the attorney has to make the decision whether to proceed with the query. If the attorney's decision is to proceed, the rest of the answer might discuss the nature and limitations of employment data and medical records, the amount of agreement (or disagreement) among the various employers and physicians, and how fallibility or validity of collateral information was judged in the process of a review of the records.

The situation may change somewhat when it is the judge who demands *yes* or *no* answers. With attorneys demanding answers, witnesses should use their knowledge of the issues and case to attempt responsible rather than simplistic answers; these efforts succeed or fail depending on the respective skill and clarity of thought of the attorneys and witnesses. Judges are a different matter. Because judges are the authoritative controllers of the trial process, efforts to place answers in context may be more difficult in reply to the court's instructions.

I testified in one jury trial in which the judge instructed witnesses actively, intervened frequently, and devoted effort and attention to being in full control of the trial process. Let me note that this judge was scrupulously fair. Unlike some judges who seem to reveal an affiliation or at least an interest in one side more than the other, this interventionist judge evenhandedly ruled or interrupted in perhaps half of the questions posed by both sides.

The cross-examining lawyer asked me if I had written the word "malingering" in the margin of my notes taken during the course of clinical interview. Indeed, I had, preceded by the word "hyp" to remind me that a particular seemingly exaggerated emotion of the evaluee had led me to make a hypothesis, not later supported, that the evaluee may have been malingering. The question was worded:

"Doctor, is this word, written in your own handwriting, on page four of your notes, the word 'malingering?' "

"Yes," I acknowledged, "but it was . . ."

At this point the judge cut off my answer with a quick, authoritative statement:

"Asked and answered."

"Your honor, the word . . ."

The judge looked at me sternly, "The question has been asked and answered."

Encouraged by this small success in an up-to-that-point fruitless cross-examination, the attorney continued to take isolated words or phrases out of my notes and my report, and to inquire whether I had indeed written them. My efforts to explain the context of those notes were met by the repeated instruction from the bench, "Asked and answered."

What should a witness do in this situation? To begin with, judges sometimes do instruct witnesses about their answers. However, no rule of law requires a witness to answer a question in any particular fashion, and according to one expert observer,[1] no legal authority exists for judges to direct witnesses to answer "yes" or "no." In some instances, witnesses may choose to tell the judge that the question does not lend itself to a "yes" or "no" answer. In many other instances, witnesses do respond to the instruction from the bench and give an answer in the requested form. At this point, witnesses may well think ahead to the redirect examination, and realize that a good attorney will correct any seriously misleading impressions from the cross-examination. By itself, that possibility should help sustain the witness. Positive and internal self-statements affirming the worth of the evaluation and findings may also help.

Nevertheless, the witness still has to deal with the immediate questioning, and some individuals experience a sense of helplessness in not being able to correct false innuendos and inferences. The case I reported left me with a mixture of reactions: unhappiness, that I was unable to speak; a clear intellectual awareness of what the attorney was doing; and a personal sense that the process was probably ineffective on its face because of the fragmented sequence of questions. As it happened, the attorney who retained me also thought the questioning was ineffective, and did not explore it on the redirect examination. I would have preferred it if he had.

This "asked and answered" example is just one of many constraints that can limit the nature and scope of witnesses' testimony. Witnesses deal with these constraints best by accepting that this is part of the court process. They may try to correct misleading impressions with statements like "you are taking my words out of context," but if such efforts fail, they should act responsively, reply honestly, and accept that being on the witness stand means that they cannot always say everything they wish.

---

[1] I am indebted to Charles Patrick Ewing for this information.

The Maxim: When the court limits what you can explain, neither panic nor become angry or defensive; rather, testify as confidently and accurately as you can within those constraints.

3

Back to One

THERE ARE MOMENTS OF ONENESS and of being naturally at home in the courtroom that can yield a gratifying ease of communication. Sometimes that ease can work in a way that allows you to share knowledge and understandings in a manner that brings out the best of who you are as a person.

Consider this example of personal ease and quick thinking that occurred when Dr. R. K. (Kim) McKinzey—an Oakland, California forensic psychologist—was testifying in an arbitration hearing to determine a disability payment.

> The patient had suffered a postconcussion syndrome after a low speed motor vehicle accident and head trauma. I was trying to explain that our sensitivity to such temporary deficits had risen in recent years. "The days of Captain Kirk getting bashed in the head without sequelae are gone" quoth I. The defense attorney (some young guy) said "Captain who?" In the astonished silence that followed, I replied, "He's a literary character." The judge loved it. (R. K. McKinzey, personal communication, 1998)

Let us introduce a hypothetical alternative response to the Captain Kirk comment. Suppose the attorney was wearing a trekkie costume (ensign insignia) beneath his suit, and he asked, "but didn't Kirk almost die when a Klingon warbird uncloaked and transported him aboard?"

Or, "Surely, Doctor, you are not drawing on this television fantasy for a frame of reference for your clinical judgment?"

The answers to those questions are straightforward. To the first, the witness might reply "As I said, TV and movie characters are banged fiercely in the head without any harmful effects. In real life, the effects can be catastrophic."

To the second question, the answer could be "That's exactly my point; one needs to draw on psychological knowledge about closed head injuries and not fantasy notions of how heroes are invulnerable to blows to the head."

The flow of the actual testimony by Dr. McKinzey could not have been predicted. That is, he certainly could not anticipate that counsel would have been ignorant about the name of the lead character in the original *Star Trek* television and movie series. This spontaneous exchange illustrates the moments during testimony when a witness is able to shed the sense of public self-consciousness from being on the stand and, instead, to be personally visible as well as professionally present. This process has been labelled by Sheldon Kopp (1977) as being *Back to One*.

The phrase *back to one* comes from meditation instruction in which the meditator is told to count from 1 up to 10 successively with each breath. Whenever a stray thought appears or a self-evaluation of how one is doing, it is necessary to go back to one. It is profoundly frustrating at first to find that you have always to go back to one. The solution, in part, is changing your frame of reference. After periods of meditation practice, a notable event occurs; evaluative and intrusive thoughts no longer appear, and the practitioners relax into the experience.

With a view to applying the experience to court testimony, read this passage by Kopp as he writes about psychotherapy:

> So it is that when the therapist does the best work, he or she does not experience trying to change the patient, or even experience doing psychotherapy. The therapist becomes the Work. The therapist is the psychotherapy and it all just seems to flow. (p. 21)

The parallel for court testimony is that witnesses are at their best when they do not try to "win." Trying to win the battles and trying to triumph do not come first. Instead, good testimony is being one's authentic professional self, and the converse, one's authentic professional self is testimony without defensiveness and phony posturing.

A paint-by-numbers kit metaphor has been used by Mark Mays (personal communication, January 8, 1999) to describe such unselfconscious and authentic testimony, without trying to change the product. The expert's job at trial is to fill in each color carefully, without concern for the completed painting. The attorney's task is to arrange the colored areas into a meaningful pattern through choices about the order and questioning of witnesses (although before the trial, experts certainly can help the attorney compose parts of the portrait). This limited scope of the expert's roles helps reduce one's excessive reach and self-demands.

The application to court testimony lies in being at ease. Let me paraphrase Kopp. In court testimony (as in psychotherapy) witnesses repeatedly show a willful attachment to how they are doing, to how the testimony is unfolding, to the results, to getting their own way. These are all distractions from testifying. The solution is to go back to one, to the fundamentals of what the witnesses know best and who they authentically and genuinely are as people.

The Maxim: Self-critical judgments and zealous attachment to the results distract from effective testimony. Seek to become authentically yourself as a professional and as a witness.

4

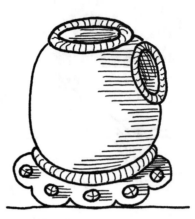

Bulletproofing

A S PART OF PREPARING THIS BOOK, I wrote to Margaret Hagen, author of *Whores of the Court* (1997), a fiercely critical polemic attack on psychology and psychiatry in court that concludes with the assertion that there has been "... a comprehensive undermining of the American legal system through the institutionalization in our justice system of the assumptions, principles, and prejudices of current psychological practice" (p. 306). I asked Dr. Hagen whether I might look at the transcripts of her brother's civil trial that initiated the writing of her book. It seemed that some exchanges between the attorneys and experts in that trial might be useful illustrations in my writing about expert witnesses. This was her reply:[2]

> Date: Fri, 23 May 1997 10:49:00–0400
> To: SBRODSKY@GP.AS.UA.EDU
> From: hagen@bu.edu (Margaret A. Hagen)
> Subject: Bulletproofing
>
> Hi,
> I was thinking about your msg. In the transcripts I

---

[2] Included here with her permission.

have of my brother's trial, two things really stand out for me. Well, three. First, it cost me $5000.00 to get the transcript made from modern, no court recorder, video courtroom, from video to audiotape to typed Word document to paper. Oy.

Second, much of the testimony is about really bizarre sounding "therapy" techniques like aqua genesis for prenatal regression. Much of it simply dumbfounded the very intelligent judge. (No jury.)

Third thing is the defendant's attorney submitted to the judge five inches of scientific papers on repression and recovery of memory which the judge actually read!!! Oops.

Fourth, that defense attorney was very successful at revealing the astounding ignorance of the young "counselor" about ANY scientific research at all on such things as memory and repression. It was not clear she knew nearly as much about Freud as she did about pink bubble imagery and pounding pillows with tennis rackets. So, the msg here is, "Do not put such people on the stand if you wish to win the case." What else? Is more than three (points). Ah, the issue of retrospective clairvoyance. "I know HE caused this trauma 20 years ago!"

Judge: "How do you know that???"

Now, all of the above notwithstanding, I CANNOT help you bullet proof these clinical telepaths against aggressive and knowledgeable questioning.

Yours,

Margaret A. Hagen

Department of Psychology

Boston University

Boston, Mass. 02215

I replied:

Hi Margaret

Actually, I would not want to bulletproof psychologists who tout iridology and aqua genesis. My belief is that it is the responsibility of the discipline, of courts, and of cross-examining counsel to tear up such witnesses into little shreds and scatter them to the winds.

Quite to the contrary of your assumptions, my aim is to aid competent and conscientious witnesses who are

unfamiliar with courtroom questioning and to keep
them from being devastated and traumatized.

Thanks for taking the time to reply. I do plan to read
your book (and not automatically accept any of the reviews as the revealed truth), as I look at other sources
I am reading, and to look for excerpts that may fit with
my manuscript.

Best wishes

Stan

This exchange illustrates how scholars and academics often
misunderstand the nature of instructing expert witnesses. It is not
about empowering the fatuous and emptyheaded. It is about empowering and educating witnesses, especially expert witnesses.
People sometimes ask me if I am doing a disservice by potentially
aiding witnesses who practice junk science or who are genuinely
guilty defendants standing trial. They miss the point of this book
and its predecessor. I do not presuppose that my writings serve
directly to promote justice, a goal that is beyond the reach of any
one individual.

In reading this draft, Margaret Hagen commented "I disagree. I think the promotion of justice is not only a reachable goal,
but a profound duty." Testifying in court should indeed promote
that aim. Teaching about testifying in court is different.

In my university classes, I never ask students whether they
will commit themselves to use what they learn exclusively for
causes of which I approve. In my expert witness workshops, I
rarely tell participants when they should and should not use these
methods. Even when my values differ strongly from the values of
my students or workshop participants, and those differences surely
appear occasionally, I do not instruct them about the substance of
their testimony (except in modest ways, now and then). If I tried
regularly to instruct on substance, I would be going beyond the
task I have taken on, and might be imposing my personal values
on them. It is the task of the adversarial process to ferret out and
expose scholarly scatology. When done well, a deposition or cross-
examination should lay bare the weaknesses in assumptions, methodology, or findings.

Note I used the word "rarely" above. What I do tell participants is that if they are unprepared, they deserve to be attacked

on the stand. When a few essentially unprepared and unknowledgeable participants say they have never been attacked, I respond that I hope they will be, if they have not done their scholarly homework. In that sense, teaching about court testimony may contribute indirectly to just outcomes. Prepared and responsible experts may be less distracted from presenting their findings and opinions.

When Margaret Hagen used the term "bulletproofing," I believe she was onto a relevant metaphor. I see expert testimony knowledge as a protective vest one can choose to don. Wearing it says nothing about the manufacturer, nor about the body inside. It is a choice available to the informed consumer who sees a risk. No vest is fully bulletproofed against opponents who are well armed, but sound scientific foundations of findings and awareness of the courtroom gambits go a long way toward protecting experts.

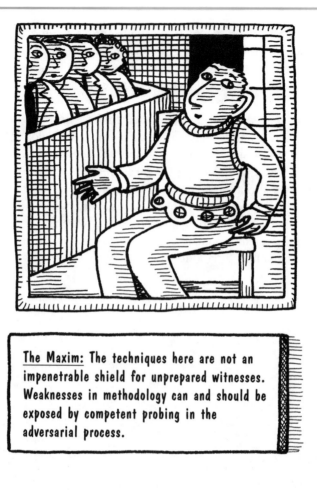

The Maxim: The techniques here are not an impenetrable shield for unprepared witnesses. Weaknesses in methodology can and should be exposed by competent probing in the adversarial process.

5

Confabulations[3]

T HE HINT THIS MIGHT BE A peculiar day began when the attorneys gathered their witnesses together to talk about the anticipated testimony, plans, and sequence of events in the hearing. Opposing counsel, the Assistant District Attorney, drifted casually into our group, offered us all coffee, and asked politely if anyone minded if he listened to the discussion. He was dissuaded. Peculiar moved to surreal during the hearing when I noticed him sticking out his tongue across the courtroom at the opposing attorneys.

The physical setting was equally strange. Gargantuan John Deere farm vehicles lumbered down the street outside the courthouse to loud applause as part of the homecoming festivities. Inside, two rows of juror chairs were lined up directly in front of the judge's bench and the witness box, while the attorneys sat at the far right and left sides of the courtroom, facing each other. The witness box had no chair. Instead, a box on which the witnesses sat was covered with a flat vinyl cushion, while a smaller cushion

---

[3] Confabulation is customarily defined as the unintentional replacement of facts with fantasies and usually refers to faulty memories or perceptions.

provided limited padding as witnesses rested their backs against the wall.

One of the expert witnesses began to make up answers. The questions were about a competency evaluation the expert had conducted with the petitioner some 11 years earlier, while the petitioner had been psychiatrically hospitalized during a recess in his murder trial. The petitioner was not in need of further hospitalization at that time, the witness testified at the hearing. When he was confronted with transcripts of his testimony to the contrary at the original trial, he said that he now guessed the man did need further hospitalization, but it was hard to tell because the man had been hospitalized only 24 hours at that point. Then he was shown documents that indicated that the man had been hospitalized for 8 days at that point, and he reversed course, and opined that enough time had passed for a proper evaluation. So it went. Every assertion he made may have fit the pattern of other defendants he had evaluated, but it became increasingly apparent he just did not remember this case, and would not admit it.

At times the Assistant District Attorney objected to the questioning of this witness, but the cross-examining attorney was given much leeway when she explained she was attempting to impeach the witness. In the heat of the cross-examination, the expert's microphone began to droop. As he sank himself deeper into a pit of confabulations, the microphone at the end of its supporting metal coil slowly tilted from being straight up and near the expert's mouth, to sinking gradually past a horizontal position, and then slowly downward until it hung limply from the coil. The expert would notice, pull it up, and its descent would begin again until it drooped straight down. This process repeated over and over. I couldn't take my eyes off the microphone. Even in the serious and intense milieu of this cross-examination, I fought against breaking out into a broad and inappropriate smile, while clenching my teeth together tightly so I would not guffaw.

What should the expert have done? First, he should have prepared. He had not reviewed his earlier testimony or notes, and went into court shooting from the hip. Well, the lip. Second, he should have been scrupulously careful about staying within the limits of what he actually recalled. At times all of us will be asked questions on the stand about events we do not recall clearly. Many experts consider it a loss of face to say they do not remember. My advice is to say exactly that: when you do not remember events, simply say so. In cases like this in which the events took place over a decade ago, it is no disgrace to forget.

Third, do not feel obliged to come up with testimony to support the side that called you. This particular expert was state-employed and always testified for the prosecution. My observation was that he searched for answers, whether factual or not, to aid the prosecution.

Fourth, he should have stopped his testimony for a few seconds and fixed the microphone coil. If he had twisted the coil up and around, the microphone would have stayed in place, as it had with all of the other witnesses.

In this same hearing I was accused of making up a key psychological construct. During a 2-day period of the original trial in 1987, the defendant had been unable to walk, bathe or dress himself, follow the proceedings, or consult with his attorney; these behaviors were in marked contrast to his alert and lucid earlier state during the trial. I described my assessment from various data sources of his functioning during those 2 days as a "retrospective" assessment of competency to stand trial.

Opposing counsel sought to develop the case that I had invented the term, that nobody else had ever done such an assessment, and that there was no foundation for such a procedure. My responses were that such assessments are rare, but not unheard of; that there was robust case law revolving around competency at an earlier time (it was true, but I am glad he did not challenge me on my legal credentials); and that the psychological criteria for competency were exactly the same whether one assesses a person today or assembles observations and various medical and institutional records from earlier years. I testified that the term "retrospective" was a descriptive term rather than a free-standing scientific construct. That seemed to work.

The lesson from these responses is to be studiously prepared. In both examples of testimony, the cross-examinations were vigorous and provocative. The attorneys' questions were good instructive vehicles because they served to challenge expert knowledge and memory in thoughtful ways. They emphasize the importance of acknowledging what one does not know and remember, and clarifying what one does know and remember. In all instances of testifying, confabulating of answers is irresponsible and deficient.

The Maxim: Never make up answers, keep your answers carefully within the context of what you know and remember, and never automatically reply within attorneys' frames of reference.

6

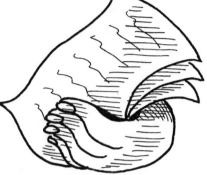

Context: 1. Choosing a Phrase

TWO YEARS AFTER DANNY STRICKLAND had killed his father and waited for a long time by his father's decomposing body, a hearing was held before a Georgia jury to determine if he was competent to stand trial. The witnesses called by the defense were mental health professionals from the Central State Hospital in Milledgeville, Georgia. Their conclusions were contested by the state and televised excerpts were shown and discussed on Court TV, allowing the expert testimony to be viewed by a wide audience. (The following testimony from the Strickland case has been edited slightly for clarity.)

This trial illustrates issues of putting testimony in context. In this chapter context refers to the art of seating testimony properly within the surrounding procedures, knowledge, and professional influences; it also means mastering isolated segments of inquiry during cross-examinations that can alter the impact of testimony.

The essential question raised by the prosecution was whether Strickland was malingering. The witnesses had testified about a number of visual and auditory hallucinations. Among other statements Strickland had made to the hospital staff was that he had heard the voice of God instructing him to keep his father from killing the Messiah, and that he had seen the face of Christ and the face of his father on the wall.

During cross-examination, the prosecuting attorney asked the psychologist on the stand, "How did you determine that Strickland was unable to understand the charges against him?"

The witness replied, "As near as I can recall, from my notes, I just asked him."

Three failures to use context successfully may be seen in this reply.

First, the phrase "As near as I can recall" is superfluous, and diminishes the power of the testimony. It is a given of testimony that experts are limited by their good or bad memories of assessments. This statement hints at poor recall of a customary aspect of professional procedure. One should always be prepared and certain about the methods used to obtain fundamental findings.

A better response would have been to declare "I used the standardized questions and procedures that I always follow: a systematic inquiry into the patient's knowledge, understanding, and ability to process in a meaningful way what it means to be charged with a capital offense."

The second phrase, "from my notes" is not intrinsically in error. Witnesses may responsibly and appropriately rely on their notes. The problem in this usage, however, is the implication that the locus of knowledge lies within the psychologist's notes. I suggest routinely reviewing and, as much as possible, committing to memory the contents of one's notes. The notes should supplement the witness's expertise, and not the other way around. The appropriate context is to see notes as tools.

Finally, this phrase was used: "I just asked him." The word "just" is unnecessary. It appears to mean "this was *all* I did." Employees at McDonald's "just ask" you what your order is. Professionals ask on the basis of the full context of their training, experience, methodologies, and conceptual understandings of the issues and behaviors at hand. Thus, a more accurate answer would be "I probed in considerable depth what Mr. Strickland knew about the nature of the charges, what the charges actually meant, and I evaluated the range of his abilities to grasp the essential issues involved, using a series of standard inquiries from both the Competency To Stand Trial Assessment Instrument and the Georgia Court Competency Test."

In this same hearing, a testifying psychiatrist related to the court a list of the various medications being administered to Strickland. He used a throw-away line in describing the benefits of Risperdal, saying "It's the best thing since, ah, Koolaid, in taking care of psychotics."

The cross-examining attorney let the remark pass. However, he might have said, "And, Doctor, just how good *is* Koolaid in treating psychotics?" I have no idea what the meaning of Koolaid was in the life experience of this particular psychiatrist. My own association is of something excessively sweet and watered-down. This statement is even more empty than the common cliche "the best thing since sliced bread," a reference to a time essentially nobody remembers.

The Koolaid reference serves as an example of *meandering context*. The witness tries to be colorful or interesting and draws on a metaphor or context that fails instantly on scrutiny.

Suppose the attorney *did* ask "just how good *is* Koolaid in treating psychotics?" I would hope the immediate answer would have been "I should not have used that description. What I meant to say is that Risperdal is among the more effective medical treatments to relieve psychotic symptoms." That answer places the medication issue back in correct context.

Sometimes witnesses slip out of context by their own unconsidered statements. Equally often, it occurs because the attorney is skilled at redefining the context. By shifting the statement or word to another issue, witnesses can be made to seem to contradict their findings or be foolish.

In her remarkable book *Individualizing Psychological Assessment*, Fischer (1994) has argued that all psychological interviews, tests, and findings need to be looked at in the context of the person's own life, milieu, and phenomenological world. Otherwise, one only has glimpses of the client's functioning. A parallel exists with court testimony. When one's language of testimony or visible life experiences slip outside of a meaningful context for the finders of facts, it interferes with credibility. Good witnesses maintain the context of their reports to the court.

The Maxim: Keep the context of your assessments and findings as a foreground issue in expert testimony.

7

Context: 2. Minor Gaps

THE FOCUS FOR MOST OF US in preparing for our testimony is to think through the presentation of the substantive issues in the case, and then the possible challenges during cross-examination. A sensible focus is to attend to the essence of what involved us in the first place, and to insure that we are masters of the core methods and findings of our professional work. It can be a distraction at the least, or a seeming failure, at the most, when attorneys do not ask major questions about a thoroughly competent assessment, but instead seek out the minor blemishes and ordinary gaps that are part of all professional work. An example of this was provided by Dr. Beatrice Norris, who is in practice in Calgary, Alberta, Canada. Dr. Norris wrote this description (personal communication, December 22, 1995):

> Fancy spending the week before Christmas on the stand, defending one's evidence in a bilateral custody assessment. Such were my experiences, and four days on the stand is considered an unusual phenomenon. . . . The retaining counsel and client told me I'd done a "wonderful job."
>
> However, in spite of one of my better court performances, I did not handle well some questions asked by

cross. One of those was if I had checked each family member about particular statements. For example, "Mr. E. told you that his ex-mother-in-law fed the family nine times out of ten in her restaurant. Did you check with his ex-mother-in-law? His wife? His son?"

This event is of minor significance, and irrelevant to the other significant allegations. The cross repeatedly questioned me whether I had checked out other family members about other irrelevant events. As you must appreciate, it is not possible to validate all statements made by the two parents in a custody assessment. The examiner can only validate allegations of serious concern. Nonetheless the cross made a point of asking questions of this nature. Do you have any suggestions as to how these questions could have been handled in an expert manner? I need to address the content more forcefully.

Beatrice Norris' experience echoes that of many witnesses, in which they are asked about procedures they could not reasonably be expected to follow. I suggest three possible routes to handling such questions. The first route has to do with your fear of being caught as a bad clinician. The feeling is sometimes "Oh, no! That is awful. I cannot answer the question, and I am therefore deficient!" That feeling of being deficient can make its way into tone of voice, posture, and content of the answer. Before any other response, the first necessary action is self-calming. Don't feel self-critical. Breathe. Sit up a little straighter. Then answer the question.

"Did you check with his ex-mother-in-law? With his wife? His son?"

An internally strong "No" may be all that is necessary. The "No" should not be presented as a confession of negligence. Rather, it should be a matter-of-fact statement without embarrassment or ego-involvement. If one is feeling especially put upon and just a little impertinent, one could respond to just one of these questions by saying, "No, why *would* I do that?" That reply gives the witness a chance to explain and briefly may shift an explanatory burden to the cross-examiner.

A second route for managing this kind of questioning is to use a form of push–pull, in which the direction of cross-examination is carried further by the witness. Let us go back to the threefold question:

"Did you check with his ex-mother-in-law?" "With his wife?" "His son?"

A push–pull reply would be:

"Not only did I not check with the ex-mother-in-law, the wife, or the son, but I also did not check with any of the aunts or uncles, any of the cousins, or with any of the customers." This response takes the momentum away from the cross-examining attorney and moves the sense of control to the witness.

The third route is to contextualize the issue. One contextualizes an issue by moving the minor problem of not asking about whether one particular relative fed the family to the two broader issues of the nature of corroboration in custody evaluations and the bottom-line conclusions about how this family worked. Thus, a contextual reply about corroboration would be "I did not seek to corroborate whether the family was fed in the restaurant or to validate what was reported about shopping for shoes or about who bought chewing gum because they were not central behaviors I used in forming my opinion."

This commitment to placing the evaluation in context is reminiscent of a fable that Jean Baudrillard (1994) used to open his book *Simulacra and Simulation.* He wrote of the map-makers who were supposed to have made a map of their empire that was equal in size to the territory of the empire. This absurd image has its parallel in the concept of custody or other psychological evaluations in which a totally complete evaluation would call for observing the entire lives of the participants. The alternative to such an absurdity is, of course, a structured and standardized system in which the important parts of the clients' behaviors are examined and corroborated.

Now let us go to the other leg of contextualizing, which is to place corroboration in the context of the overall findings. Given the same initial questions, the witness might reply, "While I did not ask anyone about whether the family did eat regularly in the restaurant, their answers would not have influenced the compelling results that these children will only flourish in the custodial care of their father/mother."

This assertion may also be made in the shorter form of, "I did not ask because it would not have made any difference in any way."

The good cross-examining attorney often seeks to put findings in an alternate context in which knowledge, methods, or conclusions seem weak. The witness's task is to keep his or her testimony both responsive and in context.

The Maxim: When minor gaps are questioned, answer matter-of-factly, and in the context of the nature of psychological evaluations and the findings of the case.

8

Daubert Hearings

WHEN THE U.S. SUPREME COURT issued its ruling in *Daubert v. Merrell-Dow* in 1993, an observer from Mars or Paris might have thought a revolution had taken place in admissibility of expert evidence into federal courts. No revolution occurred, but rather an existing path became more clearly marked.

The actual issues in *Daubert* were whether the antinausea medication Benedectin taken by pregnant women caused teratogenic disorders, specifically, foreshortened limbs, in their children. Four criteria emerged from the *Daubert* decision. With an otherwise qualified expert, these elements are necessary for admissibility of testimony:

1. *Reliability of the methodology.* It is a peculiarity of the court's decision that it used the word *reliable* to apply to what is customarily called scientific validity. It is not the opinion or finding that necessarily has to be scientifically reliable, but only the methodology or principles used to arrive at that point.
2. *Relevance.* The test is: Will it assist the trier of fact in that it is connected to the issues and facts?
3. *Reasonable reliance.* If the facts or data are not otherwise

admissible, they must be based on data of a type reasonably relied on by experts in the field.

4. *Not prejudicial.* As usual, the probative value must outweigh the prejudicial value of the testimony. Confusing, misleading, or prejudicial testimony is excluded.

So far, these criteria simply restate the 1975 Federal Rules of Evidence, which in essence supplanted the 1923 *Frye* criteria. What is new is the requirement that the judge make a preliminary assessment of whether the expert evidence is scientifically valid, and if it meets the other three criteria. In an effort to rule out junk science, the judge must assess these following guidelines for scientific knowledge:

- If the underlying theory or methodology can be and has been tested.
- If the methodology has been subjected to peer review and publication.
- If the known and potential error rates are acceptable, and the methodology meets related standards and safeguards.
- If there is widespread acceptance in the scientific community of the technique or methodology (essentially, the *Frye* criterion).

As a result of *Daubert*, experts are sometimes in a position of defending their methodology and science before a trial, or sometimes during it, always in an *in limine* hearing. Either side may request a hearing, and they are sometimes requested for strategic reasons, to look at the nature and strength of opposing witnesses. Judges have to decide whether the witnesses and evidence meet the above criteria, not necessarily an easy task given the complexity of various expert testimony on DNA evidence, among other topics. Indeed, the minority (but concurring) opinions of Justices Stevens and Rehnquist queried whether judges were in essence required to become amateur scientists. This is a fair question. I suspect that the nature of mental health knowledge and evidence, alone, may well be beyond the conceptual reach of a number of judges.

How does this affect most witnesses?

First, *Daubert* does not apply in all state courts. At this writing 23 states are *Daubert* states and at least 15 states still follow

Frye—general acceptability of the methodology—and a number of others have not embraced *Daubert* in its entirety. It is worth checking on your state criteria.

Second, not all experts are subject to *Daubert*. Some federal appellate courts and many state courts have ruled that various technical and professional experts are not subject to the full scientific reliability standard, and only to general acceptability.

I was at a meeting in which physicians stood up and indignantly asserted they should not be subjected to *Daubert* criteria when they testify about cases they have seen, because scientific reliability is not a central part of medical diagnosis and practice. Whether that assertion is true or not is arguable. However, practitioners and technical experts of all sorts should not automatically fear that they will be held to the scientific rigor of other experts. Should the expert on sulphur air pollution particulates be held to scientific rigor when controlled experiments and good science are beyond the reach of this field? Maybe. But in many courts, judges will not hold this position.

Third, it is not necessary to publish articles in peer reviewed journals to be accepted as an expert in a *Daubert* hearing, although publishing definitely helps. Few experts are seminal or definitive investigators of a topic. Publishing does not conclusively prove expertise. Some manuscripts with flawed methodologies are occasionally published because they offer conceptual or innovative insights in other ways.

For purposes of *Daubert* hearings, a substantive mastery of scientific knowledge that applies to one's methodology serves the expert well. The standard is not one's own research but rather research that supports the methodology and has appeared in peer-reviewed journals.

Fourth, some experts should be worried about *Daubert*. These justly worried experts are the ones who use intuition and experiences, giving their firm convictions and conclusions without serious scholarly confirmation. For those worried experts, I have a recommendation. Get deeply and thoroughly into the scientific literature about your expertise. I have had experts tell me there is no scientific literature in their specialties of roof leakage in building construction, in early diagnosis of childhood hemophilia, and in fundamentals of commercial pilot training. To them I say, be certain to recheck the literature! If you have not been a conscientious searcher and consumer of knowledge, you may be in danger of failing to be accepted as an expert under *Daubert*.

For all such experts proclaiming no research evidence, I suggest looking harder. It may be that there is a related or extrapolated field of knowledge to explore. Some experts read only their trade or technical magazines. No better way exists to prepare oneself for judicial scrutiny than delving into and mastering directly related scientific research. Some experts have said they do not have enough knowledge to do so; in that case, consultation with other scholars is in order.

Finally, we come to the *Daubert* hearing itself. Experts should expect the hearing to be focused on the methods and science, not the results. Judges may opt to be more active than usual in questioning and there is a good chance opposing counsel will have been prepared by their own experts to ask difficult questions.

Daubert hearings can be held in criminal as well as civil cases. Product liability cases are particularly notable for extended examination of experts for admissibility. Nevertheless, *Daubert* hearings for admissibility of expert testimony are still infrequent events. James Richardson and his colleagues (1998) studied *Daubert* hearings in 74 Battered Woman Syndrome and Rape Trauma Syndrome defenses with expert testimony. Testimony was admitted in 51 of the cases and rejected in 17 cases, largely on the basis of the credentials of the expert. In none of the opinions did the judges refer to any scientific analysis. The issue that was examined by the judges in detail was the relevance of the expert testimony to the case. Richardson et al. concluded, as I do, that judges do not want to be thrust into the role of scientific arbiter. However, it is clearly foreseeable that more judges will indeed accept this role and that more experts' testimony will be subjected to this judicial–scientific scrutiny for acceptability (Goodman-Delahunty, 1997; Goodman-Delahunty & Foote, 1995).

I have a T-shirt that has a cartoon caricature of Albert Einstein in a police uniform holding up his hand in a "stop" gesture. The caption reads "186,000 miles per second is not only a good idea. It is the law." So, too, it goes for *Daubert*. Having defensible scientific foundations for one's expert testimony is not only a good idea; it is the law.

The Maxim: Under *Daubert*, professional and scientific experts should be prepared with peer-reviewed research to defend the nature of their theories, principles, and methodologies.

9

Discovery and Discoveries

THE PROCESS OF DISCOVERY of relevant facts by each side during litigation includes explicit procedures to gain advance access to knowledge about the other side's case. For that reason, attorneys conduct depositions and request facts and documentation from experts who have been retained by the opposing side. Full discovery in civil lawsuits is relatively new within the law. Some senior attorneys describe trial-by-ambush tactics in the times before opposing counsel could always gain access to their witnesses and information. Discovery is an important process because each side proceeds open-eyed, aware (more-or-less) of the evidence that will be and should be mobilized during the trial. Skilled attorneys are thorough, systematic, and careful in their gathering of information during discovery.

I suggest that a parallel process of discovery should be pursued by experts prior to a conclusion, a report, or testimony. Thorough experts seek out information that supports both retaining and opposing counsel's perspectives. Let me describe a case in which this common, background process became a foreground issue.

It began when Dr. Blue was contacted by a lawyer with whom she had worked before. The lawyer had taken over a case from another law firm and now needed an expert on general issues regarding the psychological effects of sexual harassment. The attorney described the basic details of the case and Dr. Blue agreed to be retained. The attorney provided her with medical records, employment records, and selected parts of depositions taken from a four-foot stack of records left by the previous law firm. An assistant to the attorney prepared a summary statement of facts on which Dr. Blue could base her opinion, so she would not have to sort through the towering stack of largely irrelevant documents and depositions taken over several years. The psychological issue was to be limited to harm to the plaintiffs as a result of an alleged hostile environment. The defendants' argument was that the plaintiffs were fired for incompetence, and then conspired to charge sexual harassment.

Studying the documents and the summary of facts provided by the attorney, Dr. Blue developed her opinion, which she reported verbally. A deposition was scheduled, at the beginning of which she restated her opinion. However, as the deposition progressed, Dr. Blue found herself questioned about facts that were not in the materials she had reviewed. Attorneys for both sides heatedly argued about what Dr. Blue was qualified to answer, considering that she obviously was not aware of some facts of the case. The retaining attorney repeatedly stopped the deposition to fill in Dr. Blue about missing content and then to change the focus of her testimony. Dr. Blue found herself answering hypotheticals about facts in dispute. Her opinions seemed unclear because of the emerging new content. The deposition was continued for 3 full days. The opposing attorney was furiously angry at the firm that retained Dr. Blue for wasting his time with an expert who was not prepared to answer his questions.

At this point, Dr. Blue only wanted to end it all. Not only was she caught in the middle of a legal harangue, but she had become aware that retaining counsel had wanted to save time and money by having his expert skip over so-called "irrelevant" mountains of materials. Dr. Blue ended up equivocating about most of her opinions about the case, admitting that they were true only if she could rely on the facts and statements she had understood as uncontested. She avoided the position of defending a badly formed opinion, but did repeatedly say that she did not know, had not heard of this information, and could not say if she still maintained her earlier conclusions.

In an action unprecedented in my experience, Dr. Blue took one additional step. Because she had been so unprepared, she did not bill the opposing attorney for her deposition time. It seemed wrong to ask him to pay a substantial fee for testimony that was based on such inadequate information.

Although this example is unusual in the extent to which the expert did not examine case materials, the operating principle is common. Evaluating experts sometimes fail to examine enough case-related material.

In a similar but less devastating example when I was deposed, an opposing attorney asked me repeatedly about a one-page document that was in the lengthy case files. I had no recollection of the document. The retaining attorney finally pulled the document out of the files. Although I thought I had gone through every page, I had no memory of ever seeing this page, which now took on an exaggerated importance. The appearance of this document distracted me for a few minutes, so that I was more attentive to the possibility of a lapse in my review than I was with the questions being asked.

How does one work toward all of the case discoveries coming during the evaluation phase? Here are some steps to follow:

- Record all of the completed reviews of documents, making summary notes of the reviews.
- Organize the documents by category and date.
- Use a comprehensive history form. I use Stuart Greenberg's Forensic History Questionnaire[4] as a means of obtaining a full, detailed history.
- Gather information from collateral sources.
- Administer assessment instruments that provide structure and breadth.
- Do not accept at face value information summaries prepared by the retaining attorneys or their staff. Even if they seem to

---

[4] Available from Stuart Greenberg, PhD, Suite 608, 720 Olive Way, Seattle, WA 98132.

be fair and complete, they have partisan influences that may lead them to produce biased products.

It is impossible to know everything about every evaluee. The nature of the evaluation task is to select topics that relate to the assessment issues and to know the essential and accessible content. Nevertheless, I suggest the best way for an assessor to be truly prepared is to over-review, over-read, and double check so that discovery in depositions does not also turn out to be discovery of missed tasks or knowledge by the expert.

The Maxim: Never accept attorney condensation, summary, or conclusions as your only working materials. The expert's responsibility is to review and assess the case personally and professionally.

10

Ethics in Expert Witness Testimony[5]

IN COURT SETTINGS, EXPERT WITNESSES often struggle between autonomy and internal integrity on one hand and the demands of the trial process on the other hand. This conflict is typically seen more clearly in the actions of other experts rather than oneself. I have never met an expert who has acknowledged that he or she has been coopted or unscientific in the face of advocacy demands; it is always the omnipresent and shady "other." Four ethical goals have been identified for expert witnesses (Committee on Ethical Guidelines for Forensic Psychologists, 1991):

- assume a special responsibility to be fair and accurate;
- avoid partisan distortion or misrepresentation;
- actively disclose all sources of information;
- be prepared to distinguish between one's expert testimony and legal issues and facts.

The issue of ethical obligations of experts is an important

---

[5]Many of the ideas in this chapter were initially part of a presentation at a conference on "Ethical, Therapeutic & Legal Issues in Mental Health: The Fifth National Symposium: Mental Health & The Law," Fort Lauderdale, Florida, April 7, 1995. Norvin Richards generously served as a consultant in the development of the presentation.

topic that has not been developed fully in the literature. I propose a four-level hierarchy of witness obligations. The foundation level is your ethical responsibility *to the truth of the findings*, as you understand the truth. Regardless of other roles and pressures, your core commitment is to the integrity of what you know. Even if your findings are equivocal, the accurate presentation of the specifics, nature, and limitations of the findings are the *sine qua non* of your expert testimony.

The second level in the hierarchy is made up of your *codified obligations to the court*. The courts demand that you conform to a structure of inquiry and behavior. These demands take the form of highly organized and codified *rules* (Childress, 1989), which prohibit certain evidence or permit other evidence.

The third level is your *responsibility to the party being evaluated and to both sets of attorneys;* the attorneys who have retained you and opposing attorneys. These responsibilities are far less codified than courtroom rules and allow for a greater range of interpretation. You are obligated to be realistically forthcoming about the quality and limits of the evaluation. Your ethical testimony, then, neither conforms overly to retaining attorneys' objectives nor rallies excessively against being part of those objectives.

The fourth level of the hierarchy is your *obligation to yourself and your profession* on the stand. Under a blistering cross-examination, the natural tendency to present yourself as competent can deteriorate into defensive compromising of knowledge and findings. This level of responsibility brings out your more personal judgments of how to testify.

Conflicts between the various levels arise when you find that a specific statement is ethical on one level and not on another, so that you experience substantial discomfort. Common moral dilemmas in court testimony come from ambiguous ethical conflicts. We all struggle with reconciling the limitations of psychological knowledge with the court's demands for a black-or-white legal outcome, with the referring attorney's efforts to slant information toward advocacy ends, and, finally, with our own desire for adequate self-presentation.

These principles are illustrated by the events associated with Dr. Lenore Walker's announced agreement to testify in the O. J. Simpson criminal murder trial in 1995. The author of books and

41

articles on battered wives (Walker, 1979, 1989), and described as
". . . the mother of the battered women's movement" (Sleek, 1995),
Dr. Walker defended her decision to testify that men who batter
their wives typically do not murder them.

Two sets of accusations arose: the first around the belief that
Walker had betrayed the cause of battered women, and the second
that she was a hired gun, a bought courtesan. The first accusation
reflected the existence of a perceived ethical obligation. Walker had
frequently testified for the defense in cases of battered women who
killed their husbands. Many individuals working in programs for
battered women accused Walker of being a traitor. They assumed
she was obliged to support injured wives, and certainly not to
work with the defense for an acknowledged wife-abuser like O. J.
Simpson.

This assumed obligation falls in our schema into obligation
to other parties. In reply, Walker rejected such an activist commitment, with the critique that "The position the advocates are taking
is that psychologists are not useful unless they say the politically
correct thing" (Sleek, 1995, p. 8). Her response drew on the foundation level, about conclusions she had observed as sound and true
from her professional knowledge.

The second set of accusations came from interviewers and
from other psychologists on a psychology–law Internet list. Walker
was accused of having no solid scientific foundations for her
work—that is, that the foundation level was vacated in place of
self-serving motives. Walker was seen by these writers as accepting
the task for unjustified reasons of money or publicity-seeking.

This was an illusory ethical dilemma; the dilemma was pre-
maturely constructed (she never was called to testify). Observers
are quick to see some experts as hired guns—see both Schultz-
Ross (1993) and Brodsky (1991) for discussions of this issue. As
Rappeport (1993) asserted, ". . . we must recognize that conscientious, competent, and honest colleagues may hold opinions that
are different from ours" (p. 391). Labelling differing opinions as
unethical is rash.

Sales and Shuman (1993) identified these ethical behavior
mandates in expert witnessing: "Scientist/professionals must agree
on what are the appropriate moral principles, how they should be
weighted in any given dilemma, how they should translate into

ethical principles and standards, and how these standards should be weighted when applied to a particular dilemma" (p. 228).

Of course, there is the self-correcting mechanism of the cross-examination. Paraphrasing an Ambrose Bierce quote, this corrective feedback of fierce attack on unethical witnesses may serve as "a state of pleasurable annihilation awarded to the wise, particularly to those wise enough to understand it" (Bierce, 1911/1958, p. 91). The pleasurable part comes, of course, in using the feedback to avoid ever again being so vulnerable to attack.

The Maxim: Keep your ethical priorities in order. Attending to scientific and professional truths always comes before responsibility to the court, and these court obligations always precede responsibilities to retaining counsel and to protecting one's self-esteem.

11

Evasive Responses:
Hopeless but Not Serious

IN HIS BOOK *Lies! Lies! Lies! The Psychology of Deceit*, psychiatrist Charles Ford (1996) opens with the assertion that everybody lies. He presents a long list of contexts in which deceit takes place: for purposes of sexual gratification, in the workplace, in advertising, in politics, by physicians, patients, and, yes, by scientists. After describing instances of scientific deceit by Isaac Newton, Gregor Mendel, Charles Darwin, Louis Pasteur, and Cyril Burt, Ford affirms the widespread deception he has seen: "During my own career in academic medicine, I have repeatedly witnessed incidents or heard stories of various forms of fraud, data theft, or outright plagiarism" (p. 16).

Unlike Dr. Ford, I have rarely observed outright fraud or deceit (although I certainly have heard uncorroborated rumors and stories). However, deceit can take many forms. One of the forms that appears occasionally on the witness stand is deceit through indirection, in which witnesses answer obliquely. My observation is that most witnesses do not intentionally alter content with an awareness of lying. Most would be horrified at such a thought.

However, a self-protective mode is sometimes activated that does produce misleading or evasive answers.

It is when they are being thoroughly grilled about factual content that witnesses may find themselves giving such evasive answers. Despite the fact that they know the substance of their answers, defending themselves may take an implicit highest priority. I say "implicit" because their explicit values and commitments are almost always to full truthfulness and disclosure.

These differences may be thought of as a content versus process conflict. The experienced and competent witness gives the content without unnecessary explanation. The evasive witness shows his or her sense of being threatened by engaging in equivocation. Here is an excerpt from a deposition in a mental health related civil suit that illustrates the difference between process and content while testifying. Opposing counsel was seeking to elicit testimony about knowledge of patients' records that may have reflected inadequate treatment and asked the health professional being deposed the following:

Q: "Had no one asked you to go to the computer and get a computer history of the diagnoses and treatment of those 11 patients?"

A: "Not recently. Unless you are referring to a list I have run off in the past. If I were given that list of the 11 patients, I would have to get their hospital admission numbers first."

This answer reflects three defensive elements: The "not recently" evades answering the question. After all, the attorney did not inquire about a time frame. By saying "not recently," the witness sought to shift the focus to a side issue.

The statement "unless you are referring to" indicates that the witness was attempting to mark some space in which to maneuver. Either the witness had indeed been asked to run off the computer histories or he had not been asked to do so. Furthermore, the witness was getting ahead of the question by speaking about a list that had not been part of a question.

The comment about the hospital admission numbers was a non sequitur. It answered an unasked question about the necessary prerequisites to search out the needed information.

Let us assume that the witness had searched for the computerized histories and was uncomfortable about admitting the results. My advice would be that he should own up to the findings and reply exactly to the asked question. The nondefensive witness would answer, "No."

This answer indicates that it is not true that the witness had been asked to search for the records.

This kind of evasiveness can slip into testimony. Witnesses can be testifying in careful, responsive, respectable ways and suddenly feel vulnerable. A shift in the questioning may have occurred that makes the witnesses feel they have been caught and exposed. The instinct to cover up and protect oneself is strong. However smooth the evasion may be, it is not invisible. The court becomes aware of it, and witnesses become aware, as well.

The telltale signs are feeling pressured. Anxiety levels rise. The art of handling these moments calls, first, for identifying them, "There it is. I am getting evasive and defensive."

The next key step is ensuring that the moment is transient. It helps to discard the self-statements of having to protect yourself. So does holding the lucid thought, "Give up the defensiveness. Answer the questions directly."

This situation is one in which evasive responses are normal but not advisable. Paul Watzlawick (1983) wrote a book titled *The Situation Is Hopeless, But Not Serious* in which he addresses the phenomenon. Watzlawick wrote

> The anthropologist Margaret Mead is the author of the conundrum, "What is the difference between an American and a Russian?" The American, she said, will *pretend* to have a headache in order to get out of an unpleasant social obligation; the Russian would have to *have* the headache. . . . the Russian solution is far better and more elegant. The American, to be sure, achieves his purpose, but he knows he is lying. The Russian remains in harmony with his conscience. (p. 36)

So it is with the headache of feeling attacked or threatened by counsel's questioning. The avoidance mechanism of evasive responses is like all avoidance mechanisms. They are normal but they also keep us from confronting the headaches. The harmonious action is to have the headache, to stay with the pain and with the harmony of giving an answer one prefers not to give. It may hurt, but that is not all bad.

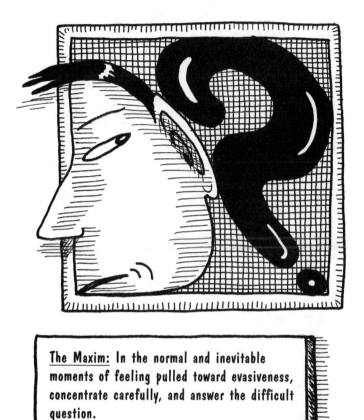

The Maxim: In the normal and inevitable moments of feeling pulled toward evasiveness, concentrate carefully, and answer the difficult question.

12

Experience Does Not Count

FOR WITNESSES TO BE CREDENTIALED as experts, the criteria in federal courts and most state courts are essentially the same. An individual may be accepted by the court as an expert on the basis of specialized knowledge that a lay person would not have. The rules of evidence explicitly mention the experience of witnesses. Federal Rule 702 states "If scientific, technical, or other specialized knowledge will assist the trier of fact to understand the evidence or determine a fact in issue, a witness qualified as an expert by knowledge, skill, experience, training, or education, may testify thereto in the form of an opinion or otherwise." One operating assumption is that experience makes a difference. In this context, the term *experience* is understood as synonymous with knowledge and expertise, much in the way that the *American Heritage Dictionary* defines experience: (a) Active participation in events or activities, leading to the accumulation of knowledge or skill; (b) The knowledge or skill so derived.

Yet, experience has emerged as a controversial issue in consideration of admission of expert witnesses, largely as a consequence of the writings of Jay Ziskin and David Faust (Faust, 1994; Faust & Ziskin, 1988; Ziskin, 1995; Ziskin & Faust, 1988). As Faust (1994) puts it, ". . . numerous studies have examined mental health professionals' experience and judgmental accuracy. Anyone who has a detailed familiarity with research should recognize that the great bulk of past and present studies run counter to the notion that more experienced clinicians reach more accurate diagnoses or predictions . . . lack of feedback and distorted feedback are probably explanatory factors" (pp. 199–200).

Indeed, Faust is correct, and in a chapter of my own, I similarly noted that experience, by itself, is unrelated to the accuracy of clinical assessments (Brodsky, 1998). A review article by Howard Garb has offered further findings about the limitations of experience (Garb, 1989). The implication of such findings is not that forensic testimony is worthless, but that skills, knowledge, and assessments specifically directed toward the legal issues at hand should be the foundations of testimony, rather than years of experience. With the development in the 1990s of considerable forensic assessment research and instruments, witnesses need not rely on experience as proof of accuracy. They can do much better by drawing on other sources of knowledge.

In the volume preceding the current book (Brodsky, 1991), I advised expert witnesses to assert that experience as related to diagnostic accuracy has scientific support. I have since retracted that statement. At an American Psychology–Law Society social hour a few years ago, David Faust marched up to me, and accused me of inappropriately defending experience. It was an unpleasant confrontation, but I did go into the literature, and now agree with the Faust and Ziskin assertions that experience appears to neither enhance nor diminish diagnostic accuracy.[6] This background discussion now brings us to the issue of how to address challenges to the worth of experience during examinations by opposing counsel or by the court. Here are three questions I posed to expert witnesses in my 1991 book:

- "Is there any substantiated scientific reason to believe that professional experience is associated with increased competence?"

---

[6]See, for example, excerpts from pages 291–293 in the chapter "Responses to Criticisms of the Fourth Edition" in Volume III of the Fifth edition of *Coping With Psychiatric and Psychological Testimony*, Ziskin (1995).

- "In fact, isn't it true that a series of scientific investigations have concluded that people with years of experience like yours are no better than untrained, unlicensed students and lay people in assessing and treating clients?"
- "Can you describe even one published scholarly report to support the belief that the sorts of experiences you have had are at all related to knowledge or skills?"

The appropriate answers to all of these questions should recognize the research. Thus, witnesses might well answer that studies have shown it is not the amount of experience that is central to doing a good assessment, but, rather, it is how skilled the assessor is and how well he or she chooses and uses measures of the issue at hand.

Witnesses do not have to be either defensive or feel defeated in any way by acknowledging the limitations of experience. It may be useful to understand the research findings in terms of a commonsense observation. Wherever one goes, one finds some people who have been doing their jobs for some time who are not especially good at it, and one finds some people who are relatively new to the tasks who are very sharp. If the meaning of experience is raised as an issue during depositions or testimony, a restatement of this observation is an understandable way of placing the research findings in context.

If the meaning of experience is not explicitly raised, it is not the responsibility of expert witnesses to introduce new topics during their testimony. There is nothing wrong with simply describing one's career experiences and letting it go at that. If individual professionals with extensive experience as well as those with limited experience are accepted by the judge as experts, and they usually are, then it is up to the jury or judge to decide what to make of the testimony.

The Maxim: Do not defend experience itself as proof of being accurate in forensic conclusions. Instead, report your career experience if asked and address the specific skills and means of reaching your conclusions.

13

Expert Witness as Master Teacher

ONE GOAL FOR UNIVERSITY faculty is great teaching. It is no accident that I say great *teaching* rather than great *teachers*, because I have come to believe that this is every bit as much a state as it is a trait. Excellent teaching is the same as excellent testifying in the sense that they are both transient situations—states—rather than necessarily and exclusively being enduring elements of a person.

Teaching and being a witness have in common that they are performance states, as opposed to states of tranquility, or of receptivity, or affection. At its best during direct examination, great teaching and testimony are the same thing.

A performance state is a relatively time-limited presentation of self that is associated with doing. It is much like my dancer friends who speak of their heightened awareness and seeking deliberate control and emphasis of certain aspects of their physical beings on stage. With masterful testifying, witnesses have a noticeably heightened awareness of how they are coming across at the moment, and they present a deliberate, controlled (but authentic) professional self.

Harold Klawans (1991), in his book *Trials of an Expert Witness*, has written,

> At trial, the major role of the expert witness is that of
> teacher. He must teach the jury what happened. What
> went wrong. What was done that shouldn't have been
> done. What wasn't done that should have been done.
> The errors of commission and the errors of omission,
> and how the errors injured the plaintiff. The extent of
> the injury. And its prognosis. (p. 152)

So far so good. Then Klawans asserts, "It's not much different from teaching medical students."

I beg to differ.

Teaching medicine or law or teaching graduate students is characterized by the unchallenged professor speaking authoritatively about content that is rarely if ever in dispute. In court that unilateral relationship of a single authority speaking to many submissive subjects (who are awaiting grades as well as knowledge) is absent. Critical examination of the content in court is present from points of view that the university lecturer would never anticipate, for three reasons. First, there are knowledgeable people ready to challenge the nature and sources of the information. Second, the conclusions are always in dispute; otherwise there would be no trial or necessity for a legal proceeding. Third, it takes place outside of the teacher's home arena. Much as visiting teams in professional basketball have much more trouble winning on opponents' courts (the 1990s Chicago Bulls' successes on the road are an exception), any expert accustomed to the rapt, note-taking acceptance of students knows that the brief, focused, and adversarial court setting makes it literally a visiting court on which the game is played.

What, then, is witness-teaching at its best? I suggest four elements:

1. *Dynamic communication.* Static presentation of findings leave to the jury and occasionally the judge the burden of making the content meaningful.
2. *Styles of relating on the stand that involve the audience.* Some witnesses have the impact of a bag of concrete mix. They need other ingredients to be useful. Ineffective witness–teachers are so wrapped up in themselves and their results that they do not connect with the courtroom audience.

Unwrapping one's knowledge with the pleasure and adventure of unwrapping holiday gifts permits the jury to feel they are part of what is happening.

3.   *Clear communication.* It is not necessary to employ the academic tool of using eight elegant words when one clear, simple word will do. If it is not understood, most of the time it will not be accepted. I say "most of the time" because sometimes cases come up in which no juror can truly understand the complexity of the issues.

4.   *Authenticity about who you are as a scientist or professional.* Witnesses who are bad teachers strain to be something they are not, and find that courtroom pressures misshape them. For all of the above advice about what to do, the overriding rule is to seek ways to be on the witness stand that present you at your natural best.

Some participants in my workshops have told me that they simply are poor public speakers. With emotion, they explain that they do not compel attention. Their voices do not carry well. They do not have the confidence it takes to speak well in front of others. In part because of an innate shyness and in part from simply being in front of a group of judgmental people, they prefer not to give talks of any kind, court testimony included.

My answer is that court testimony, like good teaching, can be the product of learned skills. One colleague in my university department was distressed to see that her course evaluations were mediocre. Instead of retreating into the hurt she felt, she sought out the best teachers in the department and several excellent teachers from other departments. She asked them to look over the ways she prepared, sit in on her lectures, and review videotapes of her classes. It meant she would hear many critical comments. However, she also took seriously the personal commitment she made to herself to become an outstanding teacher. It took about 3 years of work, at the end of which she had become a popular, highly rated, successful instructor.

Some people seem to believe that testifying well is one of the innate traits that either you have or do not have, full stop, much like the ability to mingle with members of the opposite sex and the talent to play tennis well. Not true. Quite to the contrary, courtroom testimony can be improved markedly and witnesses can become great teachers on the stand. It helps to begin with poise under pressure, good social skills, and an ease with words. Much more than that, it calls for patience, concentration, discipline, and overcoming the provincial belief that it should come naturally.

The Maxim: Part of being a great witness is to be a great teacher on the witness stand, and being a great teacher is the result of concerted effort.

14

Floccinaucinihilipilification
(flok″s*u*•nô″s*u*•nI″hil•*u*•pil″u•fi•kA′sh*u*n)

A LONG WITH THE SPECTACULAR VIEWS of the New Zealand scenery, one of the pleasures of being a visiting fellow at the University of Canterbury was the morning coffee with other faculty in the Commons Room. At 10:30 am, many of the faculty drift in, and the conversation follows unpredictable and occasionally fascinating paths. At one such morning tea, Ken Strongman spoke of learning a word that Swedes are taught is the longest word in the English language. The word is *floccinaucinihilipilification*, and the Oxford English Dictionary defines it as meaning "The action or habit of estimation as worthless."

Floccinaucinihilipilification is made by combining four separate word roots that capture that notion of judging things worthless: flocci, nauci, nihil, and pilify. I have been told by a friend, but have been unable to verify, that George Bernard Shaw constructed the word.

One way of thinking about the cross-examination approaches of certain attorneys is to understand how they are floccinaucinihilipilificators. Their means of examining expert witnesses is to seek routinely to diminish, or, at their most successful, to destroy, the apparent worth of the substantive testimony just given during direct examination.

Floccinaucinihilipilification may take these forms:

1. Diminishing the value of expert methods by comparing them with the existence of contradictory approaches in the research literature. In these cases, the questioning often begins with an inquiry of awareness of the contradicting study. It typically moves to queries about whether the methodology used in the results reported in the direct examination are equal to or superior to those of the published article being discussed.

2. Diminishing the testimony through a questioning manner that itself overflows with such sarcasm or interpersonal dismissal that the *process* of questioning is the product.

3. In a discussion of this sort, we should not forget the uses of language to restructure the understandings of the testimony. Skilled attorneys take apart the metaphors that may be used by the witnesses. They listen to word usage that is imprecise. They enter the minutiae of language to attack a witness, particularly when the substance seems unassailable.

How to deal with such approaches always starts with understanding the underlying objectives of the questions. We need to appreciate the attorney goals of arousing our insecurities. They often attempt to structure the cross-examinations and depositions to become a questioning and defending of professional worth. Once understood in this light, witnesses may feel better prepared to reply by stepping outside this framework, or sometimes by mastering it fully.

Experts who are successful in the face of such attacks begin by using methodologies that are solidly grounded in the best and most current scientific foundations. Starting from that point, they are not fazed by comparisons to other methodologies.

Next, successful experts see through the sarcastic and personal attacks. One police officer who deals with verbally abusive delinquents has described to me how he responded to taunting sexual comments about his mother: "Why, I didn't know you had met my mother," he replies. The youths' efforts to unnerve him disappear immediately. In the same sense, experts can see attorneys' attacks as similar probing for weaknesses and should stay unflustered and poised.

Finally, the minutiae of language attacks are best met straight on. If an attorney dwells on and miscasts a word like "pathological" or "anxious," the witness should feel free to say "You are using that word in a very different sense than we use in psychology," and then explain.

The process of severely demeaning the value of testimony is common. People who are faced with such framing of their testimony as worthless need to engage in clear and responsible acts of antifloccinaucinihilipilification.

The Maxim: Anticipate cross-examination efforts to portray essential elements of your testimony as worthless.

15

For Better and Worse

LYNN DARLING, in writing an article about marriage for a popular
magazine, titled her piece "For Better and Worse" (Darling,
1996). That slight rephrasing of the marriage vow from better-or-
worse to better-*and*-worse captures something about the experience of testifying, as well. Court appearances are neither always
rewarding, nor always difficult. In almost every trip to the witness
stand, there are elements of both that are present in the one ven-
ture, and certainly there are elements of both that co-exist in the
longer term experiences of testifying.

In a grand and dramatic overstatement, Darling opened her
article with these assertions:

> Marriage begins in a lie.
> It robs you of your identity.
> It thwarts desire.
> It inspires cruelty.
> It can only end in boredom.
> And yet there may be nothing sweeter. (p. 58)

She may have been writing about court testimony, just as
much as about marriage. Testifying does steal your normal identity
as a professional, as a helper, as a scientist, or as a clinician, and

gives you another, namely that of an expert witness. Of course, you still are who you are, as people who have cosmetic surgery often discover to their profound disappointment. But you also become something different: a public speaker in a literal sense, a performer, a teacher, and more.

When Darling used the phrases "It thwarts desire" and "It inspires cruelty," I was less certain of their application to court testimony, even though some aggressive attorneys draw on a deep well of unkindness and cruelty to discredit witnesses. But boredom: yes!

Witnesses who testify often, especially in commitment hearings, *habeas corpus* hearings, and other uncontested matters describe a frequent process of being on automatic pilot. The business is administrative, not confrontational. They carry on because it is their job, but there is no fear, no thrill, no adrenalin. When they attend my workshops, they often say that the challenging questions I put forth in worst case scenarios are alien to the courts in which they work.

One of the paradoxes of testifying in court is to be able to manage both the dull, repetitive tasks and the demanding, complex tasks. The dull and boring issues include the extra time and inquiries to ensure that one has indeed covered all of the necessary psychological territory, and more: that one has rescored tests to rule out simple arithmetic errors; that one has all times, dates, nature, and places of contacts recorded exactly; and that the other details of professional work are done fully, properly, and in an accountable manner. Why? To be sure, and to be extra sure. To be ready for questions, and to have a reservoir of supplemental material to draw on as needed during cross-examination, even if the attorneys never ask the questions to bring out such material, even if the cross-checking and details are superfluous in 98% of the cases.

When I bought a beach house on a small island in the Gulf of Mexico, the prior owner showed me where he had stored dozens of sheets of cut plywood that had been predrilled to fit exactly over the expansive windows, which also had predrilled holes in the frames. In the event of hurricanes striking that part of the gulf, the plywood was ready to be erected quickly. At that time there had been no hurricane in the area for 19 years, but the plywood was ready in any case. That's how it works in preparing fully for court testimony. If one testifies enough, eventually some whirlwind of an attorney will huff and puff with a hundred mile an hour wind and try to blow your testimony down. The equivalents of plywood cut and drilled in advance for protecting windows are the additional corroboration, the double checking of findings, having clients come for more than one appointment and preferably over time so a broader time sample of behaviors may be observed. All these are extra steps and preparation.

Lynn Darling closed with the thought about marriage, "and yet there may be nothing sweeter," after her list of hurts and deceits in marriage. I would argue that sweetest moments are subjective and personal to each of us. But the sweetness in doing well, really well, I mean coming out masterfully and knowledgeably in control throughout a harsh grilling on the witness stand, is wonderful. I smile now as I think back to testimony like that that happened years ago, still relishing the sense of success. The residuals of well-being mixed with competence can infuse me with warmth to this day. That is the payoff of the boredom, of insuring that the evaluation is much more than may be minimally needed.

The Maxim: Overprepare: As in marriage, personal complacency can keep you from coping effectively with courtroom strife.

16

Gender Labels

WOMEN OFTEN DESCRIBE HOW they are treated in demeaning ways when they testify. Although such gendered treatment is far from universal, it occurs with sufficient frequency that I would like to revisit this topic. The times at which professional women may be demeaned have to do with power and respect. Instead of being treated with the respect their credentials would normally elicit, a patronizing quality sometimes emerges during depositions and testimony. In courtroom settings, women attorneys as well as men may demonstrate a form of sexism with women who are expert witnesses. It sometimes takes the form of being taken less seriously than male peers. Sometimes it comes up in unwelcome comments about the women's appearance. Sometimes it appears in the ways in which the women are addressed.

For many women, a sense of helplessness occurs during these gendered exchanges. They do not want to come across as angry, for fear of undermining their testimony and raising an unnecessary fuss. At the same time, they are equally determined not to take it passively.

Consider this instance. At the very beginning of a cross-examination or deposition, opposing counsel opens with, "Hello,

Dr. Johnson. It is nice to see you today. And that is a very becoming dress you have on."

One option is ignoring the remark, and replying with, "I am pleased to be here today."

A second option is the more sarcastic "Thank you, and I am pleased, counselor, to see you are dressed so nicely for the court today." That choice makes the point that comments about clothing are out of place, but has the unfortunate byproduct of meeting inappropriateness with inappropriateness. If this reply is used at all, it is best limited to depositions.

A third option for women truly irritated by comments about their clothing is going directly to the essence of the offending comment, and to state "Thank you, but I would hope it would be my professional findings and opinions, and not my clothing, that would be of some assistance to the court today."

Gender labels refer to the terms by which women expert witnesses are called. Consider the case of Dr. Carol Holden who was testifying in a civil hearing in Michigan. She was initially called Dr. Holden during the cross-examination. As the examination moved along, the attorney began to address her more informally, calling her "Ms. Holden," and then increasingly as "Mrs. Holden" and then calling her "Carol." Because the names by which she was called were slipped into the middle of questions, fussing about them seemed awkward.

The progression of informal labels reached its peak, or nadir more fittingly, when opposing counsel called her "honey" as part of a question. Carol Holden replied:

"That's Dr. Honey, if you don't mind."

It brought down the house. It embarrassed the transgressing attorney, and it left Dr. Holden with a clear sense of commanding presence during that hearing.

What is it about the statement that worked so well? Two aims were achieved. First, the entire court understood that she was indeed "doctor." Second, she spoke within the context of the demeaning remark in such a way that she demonstrated how she could play with it without being threatened, defensive, or fragile. She jumped into the existing context, much as good therapists jump into a client's language to reframe it.

The "honey" label is one of a broad genre that includes

"sweetie," "missie," and "lady," all of which call for corrective responses that fit the individual witness's style and the qualitative
moment in the examination.

One additional term of address that is sometimes a problem
is being called "ma'm." It represents a statement of seeming po-
liteness while simultaneously avoiding calling the witness by "doctor." In Alabama, children are often raised to address their parents,
teachers, ministers, and elders as "sir" and "ma'am." Some of my
women colleagues are altogether comfortable with being called
"ma'am" on the stand and off, especially by men and by younger
women.

What should women do if they are not comfortable with
being "ma'am" on the stand? First, decide how important the issue
is for you. If the discomfort is mild and not distracting, you may
wish to let it be. If the discomfort is more than mild and is distracting, a correction may be needed. Such corrections of gender labels
that are culturally consonant and not intentionally offensive should
be gentle. Rather than firmly instructing the attorney to call you
"doctor," you may wish to say that you have a preference for being
addressed as "doctor" when you are acting as a psychologist. But
be prepared for an acquiescing "yes, ma'am."

Parenthetically to this discussion, men are sometimes addressed as "Mr." and "Sir" as a means of avoiding the more imposing "Doctor" term. The same principles apply; if there is a comfortable opportunity to correct the disrespectful use of a status
label, it should be done gently and without a hint of rancor. Charles
Patrick Ewing, who is both a law professor and a practicing psychologist, has had former law students call him "Professor" during
cross-examinations, in an effort to portray him as an ivory tower
egghead. Ewing handles it this way:

> If the cross-examiner is a former law student of mine,
> as soon as he addresses me as "Professor," I say with a
> smile, "Mr. X, I realize that you are a former student of
> mine, and I'm proud to see how much you learned from
> me, but I am no longer your professor, so there is really
> no need to address me that way."

The Maxim: In the difficult moments in which women are patronized on the witness stand, they may gain control by restating their status as doctors without being strident and within the context of the questioning.

17

Illusory Documentation

ATTORNEYS

I N THE COURSE OF CROSS-EXAMINATIONS and in depositions, opposing counsel sometimes use a variety of minimalist methods to gain a psychological upper hand over the expert witness. One such method is what I have come to think of as illusory documentation, or the apparent (but not real) presence of information and knowledge not available to the witness.

One variation is the "stack of source documents" on the table of opposing counsel. The stack is used during the trial by regularly pulling pages open, scanning, and then asking a probing question. What sorts this method from true documentation is that there are no relevant citations or sources in the towering stacks of papers, folders, books, and files. They are present only to intimidate. Their actual purpose is to convince insecure witnesses that an encyclopedic array of material unknown to them is available to undermine their procedures, knowledge, or conclusions.

Some documents have the appearance of being compelling counterpoints to the testimony of the witness. Some apparently compelling documents can include textbooks by opposing witnesses, reference works known to the witnesses but ones they have not read, and some of the Ziskin (1995) volumes. Attorneys who stack such seemingly relevant volumes turn the spine toward the witnesses; books there simply to impress by quantity are often placed with their spines (and titles) facing away.

This illusory documentation is probably most effective as an adjunct to examination questions. Consider this question to a witness who does not know how often he or she has testified. Following a process of selecting and then scanning a series of papers from several file folders, the attorney asks "Isn't it true, Doctor, that you have testified 34 times for plaintiffs in civil lawsuits in this state?"

The specificity of the numbers may make it appear that the lawyer knows what the witness does not. It is not unusual for witnesses to stumble or even to agree, both of which may be followed up by an inquiry to specify what cases these were. The obvious and better answer is to indicate that one does not know exactly how many times one has testified. What keeps witnesses from replying with the obvious answer is their belief that the examining attorney has specific documentation that they do not. Although mistaken in this assumption, they assume that saying "I don't know" in the face of the attorney's information will make them appear inept.

Sometimes illusory documentation takes the form of scientific studies that are mentioned in a question and that have some seeming relevance to the issues at hand. One may be asked if it is true, as research has indicated (the attorney is reading from a journal as this is asked), that over 50% of people diagnosed with Multiple Personality Disorder may well have other diagnoses that are more salient to their adjustment and day-to-day effectiveness and functioning. The sensible answer, of course, is "I know of no such research."

WITNESSES

I am much more concerned about illusory documentation by expert witnesses than I am by attorneys. When attorneys do it, it is a brief and transient gambit that means little in the overall judicial process. When witnesses do it, it represents a violation of one's obligation and an unacceptable tear in the fabric of the judicial process.

Observers new to expert testimony may be puzzled by the suggestion that experts do construct false sources of knowledge. Ethical experts do not. However, witnesses do construct information and the process by which it comes about is altogether understandable.

The typical representation of illusory documentation emerges when experts are challenged to support their methods or conclusions by drawing on the scientific literature. The proper action is to have established the sound scientific base before ever going into an evaluation or other professional tasks. When documentation is requested, for which answers are not obvious or easily forthcoming, witnesses sometimes state that they have seen the sources in recent issues of journals they have read, but that they cannot give the articles, or journal, or details. The element that differentiates more-or-less responsible vague documentation from illusory documentation is whether the expert is making it up.

I have seen experts on the stand and on the spot stubbornly state that they know about such articles, but they cannot cite them. For many of these fabricating experts, their voice pitch rises, their body postures indicate discomfort, and they either speak too quickly or stammer. When the attorney asks, "Can you give the court the title and author of even one of these articles that you say support this interesting idea you have," they cannot, but repeat their basic statements.

When the experts are questioned afterwards, they sometimes sheepishly admit that there really was no reference. But why would experts engage in such a fiction? The answer comes about from what else they say in these post-trial discussions; they always add that they were correct, anyway, in their assertions, even if they could not recall any articles they had read. In other words, they see the act of fabricating documentation as a minor sin, because they so believe in the truth of the overall assertions they have made.

My advice to witnesses in this situation is preventive; be prepared with sufficient knowledge of related scholarly literature. Still, no witnesses can have read all possible literature or topics that may be queried in court, and reporting such an impossibility is part of a reasonable response. If witnesses begin to construct imaginary sources, I would hope opposing counsel would fiercely and persistently pursue the question of how the witnesses know what they claim to know.

The Maxim: Do not construct illusory support for opinions or methods, and do not be intimidated by such illusory constructions by attorneys.

18

Inflammatory Questions

O NE DILEMMA THAT FACES testifying experts is how to respond to questions that insult and demean them. Even experts who normally present organized, clear, and scientifically sound testimony can find themselves upset when faced with an attorney who personalizes the examination. A few experts find that their own natural style of not taking insults from others leads them to become explosively angry or decidedly rattled when they are demeaned in this public forum. It is much like the 1980s film trilogy *Back to the Future* in which the lead character Marty McFly, played by Michael J. Fox, manages himself masterfully in the future and past except when he is accused of being a coward. In *Back to the Future II*, Marty McFly refuses to join in a crime, and his antagonist Griff insults him:

> Griff: "What's wrong, McFly, chicken?"
> Marty: "What did you call me, Griff?"
> Griff: "Chicken!"
> And a fight ensues.

Later in the film, Biff (a character variation on Griff) challenges him.

Biff: "Let's have it out, you and me, right now!"

Marty: "No thanks."

Biff: "What's the matter? Where you going? You chicken? That's it, isn't it? Nothing but a little chicken!"

Marty: "Nobody calls me chicken."

In *Back to the Future III*, the accusation is that Marty is a yellow belly, he replies that nobody calls him yellow, and, again, a brawl develops.

In those instances, the main character at center stage repeatedly lost control when insulted and then he acted foolishly. So it goes as well for unwise expert witnesses who find themselves insulted and unfairly questioned.

In his book *Effective Expert Witnessing*, civil and environmental engineer Jack Matson (1990) wrote about the use of inflammatory words in depositions and cross-examination. Inflammatory words are, as the name suggests, ones that stir your passions and interfere with an otherwise cool composure and presentation. These words are to experts what "chicken" was to Marty McFly. Inflamed witnesses are similarly ready to fight back, to criticize the attorney, and to deny heatedly the accusation. The fiercer the denial and fighting back, the more the expert becomes seen as vulnerable and unsteady. Let us look at some of the inflammatory questions Matson (p. 71) presented in his book that was aimed at engineers, chemists, and technical specialists. His questions presume that opposing counsel has just elicited an admission from you of something you have not done or some small mistake that you have made, admissions that are common in expert testimony.

"Doctor, you mean you spent all this time and effort on the case and totally ignored this important piece of evidence?"

A weak answer would be to say "yes." Such an admission agrees with all three parts of the question: that a great deal of time and effort was spent, that information was totally ignored, and that what was ignored was truly important. A better answer is "yes and no," with a subsequent explanation. A simple "no" may be effective because the answer to the follow-up question would be that you did indeed spend considerable time and effort, and that all evaluations are always focused on some topics and not others, or that no important information necessary to form an opinion was ignored. The same content could be given in the form of an admit—deny, in which the parts of the question that are true are acknowledged and the untrue parts are denied: "Although it is correct that I spent much time and much effort in this case, it is absolutely incorrect that I totally or even partially ignored any important information I needed to come to my conclusions."

Matson (pp. 71–72) then offers these four other questions:

> Q1. "This mistake you made . . . how many more mistakes are there in your work?"
> Q2. "Could it be, Mister, that you are flat wrong?"
> Q3. "Sir, you really don't know what you are talking about, because you didn't bother to check?"
> Q4. "You just blew it, didn't you, Doctor?"

Answers that do not work well are ones that rule out the possibility of errors and are phrased in absolutist terms. I have seen experts give arrogant and absolutist replies like these:

- "I do not make important errors. Ever."
- "Not one mistake. I know exactly what I am taking about."
- "I am flat right and you are flat wrong."
- "I blew nothing. I resent your implication that I did."

The last question—Q4—is the easiest to handle. Matson's suggested reply is:

- "No. There was a minor error, but it had a negligible effect on the results, for the following reasons."

In responding to any of these accusatory questions, placing the error in context serves the witness well. Thus, a witness might reply to any of them as follows:

"Although there was a clerical error in not reviewing the medical records for that month, the evaluation clearly and consistently pointed to Mr. Robertson having suffered lasting and severe psychological impairment as a direct result of his accident at the factory."

Intemperate witnesses may be caught in a whirlpool of emotional overreactions, a process that almost always reduces their credibility. Poised witnesses can effectively address these forms of name-calling and accusations.

The Maxim: Inflammatory questions are best answered with calm explanations that demonstrate a confident sense of professional competence. Don't heat up on the stand.

19

Integrity Checks

IN MY DISCUSSION OF THE PULL to affiliate with the side that calls us to testify, in my earlier volume (Brodsky, 1991), I described three ways of staying objective. The first was to be aware of the pull to affiliate. The second was to evaluate the degree of personal and emotional commitment to the outcome. The third was to calculate an objectivity quotient, in which one would divide the number of cases of agreement with the retaining attorney by the total number of cases. In a footnote I reported that I had read years before about an Integrity Quotient like this, but that I could find the reference in neither memory nor my files.

Several readers were kind enough to write and supply the missing information. Robert Kurlychek, who is a clinical neuropsychologist in Oregon, not only recognized the reference to the writings of his friend and mentor Edward Colbach, but Dr. Kurlychek generously sent me a photocopy of Colbach's original article from the 1981 volume of the Bulletin of the American Academy of Psychiatry and the Law.

The beginning point for Colbach (1981) was that utmost integrity and care should accompany expert entry into the courtroom. Colbach described two measuring devices he developed to check on his integrity: a *Contrary Quotient* and a *Validity Quotient*.

For his Contrary Quotient (CQ), Colbach sought ". . . to directly attack the idea that all psychiatric experts are hired guns for whichever side asks for an opinion" (p. 286). He selected 50 consecutive criminal responsibility assessments he had conducted over a 2 year period, 29 at the request of the prosecution and 21 at the request of the defense. He assumed that the prosecution would like an opinion of criminally responsible at the time of the offense and the defense an opinion of not responsible. His opinion was contrary to the preference of the requesting attorney in 19 cases (and affirmative in 31 cases). Thus, he did not give the attorneys what they wanted in 38% of the criminal cases, and this outcome was labeled as his CQ.[7] Then Colbach examined his findings in another 50 cases, this time for personal injury evaluations, and he reported a CQ of 28%.

Colbach touched another theme in expert witness concerns when he developed his Validity Quotient (VQ), which is calculated by dividing the total number of court decisions into the number in which the court decision and his opinion agreed. Thus, if the court and Colbach agreed every time, the VQ would be 1.00 (or 100%). If the court and his opinion were in accord half the time, his VQ would be .50. The problem with this concept is the assumption that the validity of expert opinion is affirmed by legal standards as demonstrated by the court decision. I would argue that a court judgment should be considered neither to validate nor invalidate an expert opinion. After all, much more than our opinions go into the triers of facts making a judgment, including legal issues beyond the scope of our work, the idiosyncrasies of the judge or jury, and the skills of the competing attorneys. The CQ, in contrast, expands how we think of our accountability.

The idea of having a Contrary Quotient to present during challenges to one's integrity is terrifically appealing. After all, this issue is often pursued by opposing counsel anyway. The questions

---

[7] Of course, a quotient is actually the numeral result of the division of one number by another. Thus, the Contrary Quotient would be .38, and a score of 38% of opinions not in agreement represents a transformation to a percentage.

often begin with inquiries into how many cases one has testified in or been deposed. Most experts can give an approximate number. The next series of questions address how often one has testified for the plaintiff or defense in civil cases or prosecution or defense in criminal trials.

Most experts tend to be retained more often by one side than the other, if for no other reasons than word-of-mouth reputation being spread among attorneys doing similar kinds of work, and because psychologists testify much more for the defense than the state in criminal trials. Furthermore, cross-examination questions rarely ask how many times one's opinion has not been the desired outcome of retaining counsel. Consider what you would say in reply to the following question:

"Doctor, how many times have you testified for the defense, as in this case, and how many times for the plaintiff in personal injury cases?"

An answer that hints of partiality would be "I have testified for the defense in every case but one."

A much stronger answer would be to present Colbach type data, stating, "I have calculated just how many times I have come up with an opinion that supports the case of the attorney who retained me. In 50 consecutive cases over a 2 year period, I found my opinion was in agreement 78% of the time, and in disagreement 28% of the time."

What should a witness do if she or he does not have such data? The honest answer for most witnesses is this:

"Of course I am only called to be a witness when my opinion fits with the case of the retaining attorney. For attorneys to call me otherwise, when my opinions differ from their case, they would have to be desperate or incompetent. Most of my disagreements never make it to court, and almost all my agreements make it to court."

Individuals who are regularly called to testify might well try to calculate a Contrary Quotient. However, it is not always easy to categorize one's opinion. Here, as an illustration of this difficulty, is my scoring of 10 of my recent assessments:

Type of case	Retained by	Opinion for	Comment
Criminal	Defense	Unclear	Personality assessment Issue was suggestibility
Civil	Plaintiff	Plaintiff	Malpractice issues
Civil	Plaintiff	Plaintiff	Treatment of psychotic prisoners
Civil	Defense	Defense	Sexual harassment
Civil	Plaintiff	Defense	Sexual harassment Based on my report, plaintiff's counsel accepted small settlement
Criminal	Defense	Prosecution	Criminal responsibility
Criminal	Defense	Neither	Competency to stand trial: Recommended inpatient observation No opinion
Civil	Plaintiff	Plaintiff	Sexual harassment
Civil	Plaintiff	Plaintiff	Prison conditions: Judge cut off time for plaintiff's case before I could testify
Civil	Plaintiff	Neither[8]	I offered an opinion that it was a poor investment to get a full psychological evaluation

If I count the "neithers," the "unclear," and the one simple contrary opinion, my CQ would be based on 4 differences out of 10 opinions, or a CQ of .40 and a Contrary Percentage of 40%. These instances do not include the many cases in which attorneys have asked my opinion of whether they might have a case, well before any assessment. Sometimes I have asked that they send me their case materials, which I review for a flat fee for 2 hours work. Then I give them my judgment of whether the case is worth pur-

---

[8]The two "neither" opinions are probably best thought of as being contrary, because the retaining attorneys did not get the expert opinions they had hoped. In one case I was still asked to testify.

suing, and whether they do indeed want to engage me. When I offer a negative opinion, sometimes they settle or plea bargain, and sometimes they keep looking for other experts. Whatever they do, I drop out of the case at this point, often with the appreciation of attorneys who say that this saved them considerable time, trouble, and expense. Of course, the materials may not always allow even a preliminary opinion, in which case I suggest an assessment.

It is possible to aggregate these experiences to calculate a testimony percentage. That is, one may record how many times one testifies in depositions or trial for retaining counsel and divide it by the total number of times retained. This percentage or quotient is likely to be relatively low, and it has the advantage of potentially opening up a discussion of evaluations that differ from the aims of retaining counsel.

Should you develop a CQ for your own work? It is by no means a professional mandate. If you do choose to calculate your CQ, I would hope you would not do it primarily to protect yourself on the stand against adversarial questioning, but rather because it is a useful piece of information. If self-protection is the primary motive, an experimenter effect may slant the results towards the finding you seek, namely, a high CQ. If self-knowledge is the motive, then you can enter into this kind of calculation with a more objective approach and reliable estimate.

The Maxim: Challenges to one's impartiality may be addressed by having calculated (for intrinsic reasons) the percentage of times one's expert opinions are contrary to those of retaining attorneys.

20

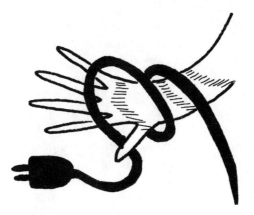

Internet Vulnerabilities

IN A RECENT INTERNET discussion of coping with Ziskin-prepared cross-examining attorneys (Ziskin, 1995), I posted playful definitions of being Ziskinized, including the quip that being Ziskinized on the witness stand represents "a natural antidote to clinicians engaging in rapturous contemplation of their own skills."

My pleasure at the remark was short-lived. Most of the time I forget within minutes such fanciful comments, but at that time I had a more enduring thought: What if a cross-examining attorney used the remark against me? After all, electronic postings are mostly public, are archived, and (with a few exceptions) are available to anybody who has Internet access and knowledge. Furthermore, they are often copied and reposted in other forums, actions over which the contributor has no control and usually no knowledge. It is not far-fetched that one's witticisms on-line may end up in the hands or files of opposing counsel. Such a possibility becomes more likely in important cases in which other psychologists consult to help opposing counsel prepare a cross-examination or a deposition.

The scenario could well go this way.

"Doctor, isn't it true that you wrote in 1998 that clinicians engage in rapturous contemplation of their skills while they are on the witness stand? And, are you doing that just now?"

The first and obvious option for preventing vulnerability to such questions is to follow this draconian rule: *Never write anything for public consumption that you are not prepared to defend in a professional context. Quips, playfulness, and professional irreverence belong in personal contacts and not on the permanent record.* Ah, but what a loss that solution would be. The electronic forums to which many practitioners and scholars subscribe are more often informal exchanges with heat and wit than they are carefully crafted expositions of scientific opinion. It is this informality that makes them fun. Just as psychotherapy clients' humor about their problems can allow perspective and even mastery of otherwise unmanageable life demands, so can scholarly humor allow us to avoid being captured by grim and somber approaches to our work. The rule offered above would work just fine for preventive and self-protective purposes; indeed, quite a number of forum members do keep the public nature of their humorous and serious commentary clearly in mind, and limit severely what they contribute. Attorneys who read the forums sometimes warn contributors to the list about the hazards of reporting specific case information as part of seeking information from colleagues.

In addition to being virtuous censors of our public utterances, an additional choice is to place our remarks in context. We tend to feel caught or trapped when attorneys turn such remarks against us. Instead, we may reply by placing them in the context of the discussion and their meaning. Replaying the question posed above, such an answer would be

"Doctor, isn't it true that you wrote in 1998 that clinicians engage in rapturous contemplation of their skills while they are on the witness stand? And, are you doing that just now?"

"Yes, of course, but that was wit, not dogma."

Most attorneys would not pursue that brief reply, not if they know traps when they hear them.

Another response might take this form: "I would hope that you would not take seriously for a second my playful remark about clinicians engaging in rapturous contemplation of their own skills. Quite to the contrary, it is critical and accountable contemplation of clinical skills that is necessary for the responsible clinician."

Still another response might be "I wrote about rapturous contemplation of clinical skills as a warning to guard against such behavior on the stand."

For me, these kinds of questions are not theoretical. In the chapter titled "While Lawyers Fuss" in *Testifying in Court* (Brodsky, 1991), I wrote about my personal way of managing the long delays while lawyers debate issues of procedure or evidence with each other. I whimsically described how I left my body, floated above the courtroom silently observing the players, and then returned to my seat when the attention of the court returned to my testimony. The first time I was aware of this chapter as a target for attack was in Ziskin (1995), who wrote:

"Lawyers have suggested that any witness who cites Brodsky as a reference should be confronted with or asked to read this particular statement and then be asked questions such as, 'Doesn't Dr. Brodsky seem to be up in the air?' or, 'Do you think maybe Dr. Brodsky needs to come down to earth?'" (Vol. III, p. 286).

This kind of query may be directed against comments made during depositions, against jokes made during convention presentations, or against any remark accessible to counsel. Assuming the court allows such questions, the answer calls for reframing. I would reply, "The section of the book you are quoting from has nothing to do with advice to leave bodies, but rather it is part of entertaining the reader who is being presented with serious and challenging issues"; or "The point was to relax when your attention is not needed, so that witnesses can conserve their energies for the arduous moments on the stand"; or "Don't be silly. Of course, I do not leave my body"; or "It is no more serious than the New Mexico legislation that proposed that all psychologists who testify in court shall be required to wear a cone-shaped hat at least two feet high, decorated with stars and half-moons, and shall accompany their testimony with sweeping gestures of a wand."

The message of my story from "While Lawyers Fuss" was that witnesses do not have to be deeply involved in all of the sidebars and minutiae of legal discourse. It is a time to recharge. Nevertheless, I wish I had written this imaginary episode with qualifiers that it was not to be taken literally. As written, the story has been more a distraction than a help.

The Maxim: When confronted with your own fanciful and playful remarks, place them in context as fanciful and playful.

21

It Would Be So Nice
If You Weren't Here

I N HIS AUTOBIOGRAPHY Charles Grodin (1990) wrote about filming
the 1974 movie *11 Harrowhouse* on location in London. With
his costar Candace Bergen, he was taking a break and lounging in
an adjacent empty room when a very snooty woman asked if they
had permission to be there. No, they replied, they did not have
permission.

"In that case," the woman responded, "it would be so nice
if you weren't here."

Grodin used this line as an underlying theme about his difficulty getting into show business, as well as the title of his autobiography. For expert witnesses, however, the statement reflects
the experience they sometimes have of how much nicer their lives
would be if they were not there in the courtroom. Furthermore,
skilled attorneys can make witnesses feel as if they are just as unwelcome as Grodin and Bergen were made to feel. The techniques
used by attorneys are chiding and shunning within unfamiliar
frames of references.

By chiding, I refer to a mild form of scolding, a manner that
expresses disapproval without actually making disapproving state-

ments. The process involves disapproval by indirection. It may take the form of a cross-examining or deposing attorney having read a report, and then asking a question to which the answer is known:

"Surely you did request and study the medical and performance records for those four years of Ms. Sergeant's life?" or

"Isn't this test you used, the Rorschach Inkblots, looked at with disdain and contempt by a large number of other licensed, board-certified, reputable psychologists?"

The closest noncourtroom parallel I can think of is when my wife tries on underwear in a shop dressing room, and I stand in the lingerie department waiting for her. I know I am in a foreign environment in which I don't speak the language and am viewed suspiciously by the natives. Surrounded by lacy constructions that women shoppers are holding up and examining, I do not belong and, at times, expect to be chided about voyeuristic activities. In this situation, I do just what witnesses may try when feeling out of place and scolded; I act as if I have a perfect right to be there, and present a calm, matter-of-fact demeanor. When attorneys chide witnesses on the stand, they continue only if it appears to have any effect. If the witnesses are unaffected and calm, the attorneys stop.

Shunning refers literally to the process of deliberately avoiding another person. The phrase used in Britain for shunning another is "Sending him/her to Coventry," which means having nothing whatever to do with a person who has acted offensively. William James captured the feeling of being shunned carried to its interpersonal extreme when he wrote in 1890,

> No more fiendish punishment could be devised, were such a thing physically possible, than that one should be turned loose in society and remain absolutely unnoticed by all the members thereof. If no one turned round when we entered, answered when we spoke, or minded what we did, but if every person "cut us dead," and acted as if we were nonexisting things, a kind of rage and impotent despair would ere long well up in us, from which the cruelest bodily tortures would be a relief. (pp. 293–294)

Setting aside that grand Victorian rhetoric, in its courtroom usage shunning has the more specific meaning of the audience rejecting our views. The experience sometimes leaves us feeling as if the questioner does not care what we say or think. Does, as William James wrote, rage and impotent despair follow? Only rarely does rage overtake us. Impotent despair is much more likely and may overwhelm witnesses who feel that their every answers are substantially and demeaningly discarded. One question that comes about in considering this sense of imminent despair concerns the locus of discomfort. Does it originate from the act of being shunned by the cross-examining attorney or does it come from within us? The question does not necessarily have a single answer. However, Arnold Buss (1980, 1988) has developed a conceptualization of such reactions that applies directly to the individual differences in response to being scrutinized and shunned on the stand.

The people who are highly anxious when scrutinized have been described by Buss as having high public self-consciousness. They answer *yes* to statements such as "I am concerned about what other people think of me," or "I usually worry about making a good impression."

When individuals have high public self-consciousness, they are likely to be overreactive to aggressive questioning of their findings and to feel they are inadequate in replying.

In contrast, individuals with high private self-consciousness have their major self-judgments come from within. They know themselves well, and are reflective, often warm people. They typically agree with the following statements about themselves:

- I am generally attentive to my inner feelings.
- I'm alert to changes in my mood.
- I'm aware of the way my mind works when I work through a problem.

In essence, such people know themselves well and trust their feelings. As a consequence they are less likely to feel shunned and chided, and instead respond to their own inner assessments of what is happening. They may think they would rather not be there, but the source of such conclusions is from a well-honed awareness of who they are, how they act, and the ways in which they have learned to assess their testimony. On the other hand, the effectively shunned witnesses are those who are primed to accept the interpersonally (in terms of personal-professional opinions in court) rejecting behaviors of opposing counsel.

Both sets of reactions may be thought of as a mixture of temporary states of processing of information and questioning and longer term traits we carry with us. For witnesses with high public self-consciousness, it is a far harder path to tread because of their own readiness to accept critical judgments.

The Maxim: Whether it indeed would be nicer if one were not on the stand comes powerfully from the sense of shunning imposed by the attorneys and the witness's own internal self-assessments. Our transient self-judgments in response can be shaped and aided by experience and successes.

22

Language:
It's a Virus

IN ONE OF THE ALBUMS by performance artist Laurie Anderson, she sings a song titled "Language: It's a Virus," which opens with the paradoxical statement "Paradise: It's exactly like where you are right now, only *much, much* better." The use of language by attorneys (and sometimes by expert witnesses) can have some of that same skewed danger and appeal. Sometimes when an attorney asks a question that loads my response in a particular direction, I find myself with an inner smile. And when the question includes three or four levels of meaning, that inner smile sometimes makes its way out into view.

Consider this example: You are testifying about termination of parental rights because of child abuse, or perhaps simply testifying in a custody dispute, when the opposing counsel asks, "Is there anything sweeter and purer than a mother's love for her child?"

The question taps into several levels. At one level, it is an affirmation of the worth of motherly love. Who could disagree? At a second level the question is posed in superlatives that are philosophical in nature. At still another level, if we assume you have been testifying that the mother has poor parenting skills with her child, it seeks to elicit a statement that in some way supports the mother's case. Let's go back to the question:

"Is there anything sweeter and purer than a mother's love for her child?"

A flip answer is possible: One could reply with the query, "Are you including mocha fudge almond ice cream in the possibilities?" This reply attends to the sweetness issue. However, flip answers are risky in court. Flip witnesses are little liked and less believed.

One might respond instead, "No. Nothing at all," and wait to see where the attorney goes next with this line of inquiry.

If your immediately preceding testimony has been that the mother has significant deficits as a parent, the responses could be "Your statement does not apply to this mother," or "Sweet and pure does not accurately describe this mother's relationship with her children."

There is a fourth alternative I like, which would be to re-frame the question by replying, "Are you asking me as a psychologist?"

The attorney's answer almost always would have to be "yes." After all, it is only as qualified experts in our field that we are allowed to testify about our opinions. As part of this reframing, a dispassionate answer would be that theologians and philosophers are the ones who would have to address the abstract issue of which emotions are most pure.

This example is representative of a large category of language viruses that call for quick triage. Language is a tool for play and for purposeful aims. It is a virus if we are vulnerable to viruses at that moment. A witness goes a long way toward invulnerability by listening with care, processing the information quickly and well, and making a choice of replies from a large repertoire of possibilities.

The Maxim: Listen well: To ward off language viruses, you need to be "much, much better" at discerning meaning of words and phrases.

23

The Last Word

WHEN CHILDREN ARE TEASED, they are often left feeling helpless and worthless. For children with disabilities or physical disfigurements, the teasing frequently builds on what is a sense of personal alienation and separation from others. In children without disabilities, as well, teasing can be a destructive experience that causes permanent scars. When I conducted research with adults about the cruelest experiences they can remember ever being subjected to (Kemp, Brodsky, & Caputo, 1997), it was common to hear about them being teased about their names, appearance, or behaviors. What Jane Kessler (1982, also summarized in Brodsky, 1988) has advised is that children being teased need to be taught how to close the teasing. No matter what the prior statement, no matter how much the last response may not seem to fit, the children are instructed to get the last word. Doing this makes them feel as if they have a weapon to use and allows them to feel more in control. It gives them a tool in what is otherwise a situation of helplessness. On some occasions, the same principle may apply in court testimony.

Elizabeth Henderson, a Canadian psychologist, attended a tutorial I led in Calgary. She described a series of discouraging events that she had experienced during a cross-examination in which the lawyer had attempted to minimize the impact of her testimony during the cross-examination:

> The lawyer had been aggressive during cross-examination and began to state "indeed!" with a nasty tone and a dismissive, sneering manner in order to have the last word after my responses. I began to get annoyed with this and decided to use oneupmanship by stating firmly "that is correct" after her dismissive "indeed." So, it would be my firm and confident tone that would be last heard with all my responses. She stopped her "Indeeds!" shortly after that. (personal communication, May 28, 1995)

Dr. Henderson's situation was an unusual one. The lawyer's statement of "indeed" has a declarative quality mixed with a questioning quality, and it was the implied questioning that permitted Dr. Henderson to get into the process and take control.

Two lessons emerge from this event. First, the attorney acted by making an explicit verbal evaluative comment, which is an uncommon event. Second, the lawyer spoke in a context that permitted the witness to continue to engage in testimony. Alertness for turning around the semantic flow is what gave Dr. Henderson the chance to get into a continuing dialogue and to make a difference on the stand.

Of course, other options are available for such situations. Some witnesses can emotionally rise above the put-downs by the attorney. Other witnesses who find themselves tempted to be competitive and petty when faced with these tactics will need to be simply and confidently professional. Nevertheless, situations do arise when making the last statement fits with the context of the questioning and promotes better testimony.

The Maxim: When the attorney comments on one's testimony, having the "last word" can empower the witness and reduce a sense of helplessness.

24

Lawyer Bashing

THE FOLLOWING APOCRYPHAL TRIAL TRANSCRIPT so captured mental health professionals' attitudes towards lawyers that it was circulated widely among groups of professionals who frequently appear in court.[9] In its entirety, the story read this way:

> An excerpt from an actual transcript:
>
> Attorney (A): So, doctor, you determined that a gunshot wound was the cause of death in the patient?
>
> Doctor (D): That's correct.
>
> A: Did you examine the patient when he came to the emergency room?
>
> D: No, I performed the autopsy.
>
> A: Okay, were you aware of his vital signs while he was in the hospital?
>
> D: Yes. He came in to the emergency room in shock and died in the emergency room a short time after arriving.
>
> A: Did you pronounce him dead at that time?

---

[9] I am grateful to Kathy Horne who spotted this transcript and sent it to me.

D: No, I am the pathologist who performed the autopsy. I was not involved with the patient initially.

A: Well, are you even sure, then, that he died in the emergency room?

D: That is what the records indicate.

A: But if you weren't there, how could you have pronounced him dead, having not seen or physically examined the patient at that time?

D: The autopsy showed massive hemorrhage into the chest, and that was the cause of death.

A: I understand that, but you were not actually present to examine the patient and pronounce him dead, isn't that right?

D: No sir, I did not see the patient or actually pronounce him dead, but I did perform an autopsy and right now his brain is in a jar over at the county morgue. As for the rest of the patient, for all I know, he could be out practicing law somewhere.

Like most readers of this story, I chuckled at the image of the brainless lawyer, and I shared the story with some friends who testify in court. Furthermore, I have tried unsuccessfully to authenticate the story. Some tales of this sort are the equivalent of urban myths and establishing their truth is difficult.

After the moment of pleasure at this story, I would like to move to the more serious issue of disparaging humor that is directed at attorneys. These days one less often hears jokes directed at racial and ethnic minorities, but jokes about lawyers continue unabated. Without repeating what seems to be an endless wellspring of jokes and without speculating about the psychological reasons for such attacks, let me note that jokes about lawyers characterize them as greedy, dangerous, dishonest, absorbed in themselves and their professions, unfeeling, and stupid. I have missed some traits, but this partial list gives a clear sense of the nature of common lawyer-bashing humor.

The issue is not whether we should ridicule lawyers (although my own opinion is that it is overdone and crude, and I am tired of lawyer jokes). The issue is whether it should be practiced in court as a throwaway line to deflect a line of questions.

Remember that many of the main participants in the court

process are themselves attorneys. Judges are almost always attorneys. The primary actors are attorneys, except for witnesses and jurors. Of course, attorneys love to tell each other lawyer jokes, but when they are told by other people, there is potential for sensitivity and an unpleasant reaction. Think of it in terms of racial epithets; they are rarely acceptable when made by outsiders and rarely offensive when made by members of the ingroup.

Let us go back to the initial exchange in which the doctor states "... his brain is in a jar over at the county morgue. As for the rest of the patient, for all I know, he could be out practicing law somewhere."

Did it work? Perhaps. But if it worked, it was in part because the doctor was reported to be a known and respected physician who could bring off this quip. If this was a jury trial, the jurors may well have enjoyed the break from the often grim exchanges in examination of medical testimony. However, it may not have worked at all if this were a bench trial; the judge may have experienced a Queen Victoria type of disapproval ("We are not amused").

In the give and take between attorneys and expert witnesses, opportunities often arise for experts to snipe at the legal profession and the personal qualities of lawyers. My advice: mostly resist, and if you do go ahead, proceed with care. Think of what it would be like to have your own profession, in the arena in which you practice, described as brainless. Lawyer-bashing on the stand is like intensive, complex brain surgery: risky, rare, but sometimes it works out okay. It works when one targets a process, such as tedium and time delays, that all observers would agree is irritating. It does not work in the typical cases in which the humor is caustic or personal.

The Maxim: Avoid antilawyer jokes and quips on the witness stand. They are high-risk comments, to be reserved for rare and exactly fitting moments.

25

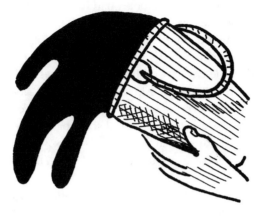

Lay Witnesses

THIS QUESTION WAS PUT to a New Zealand prostitute who was testifying in a court trial about her rape by a client: "Isn't it true that you are often paid to be bound and gagged and then stay passive and helpless while a man takes you sexually?" The question, among others, led to the audiotaped (for later distribution) meeting about court testimony I led with four members of the New Zealand Prostitutes' Collective and an associated attorney.

My introduction to the collective was through Anna Reed, a sex worker—the preferred term for prostitute in New Zealand—and head of the Christchurch branch of the collective. Prostitution is legal in New Zealand, although soliciting is not. The sex industry in Christchurch is flourishing and public, with about 2,000 women and a few men active through massage parlors and street work.

Anna is a medium height, brown-haired woman in her 50s whose life history interview was featured in the book *Working Girls* by Jan Jordan (1987). In the book as well as in person, Anna comes across as vibrant, outgoing, and warm. She bursts with good will and speaks about her sex work as expressive moments of love. Without that caring, she says she would give up the job.

Anna and I met because my wife had been doing research on the remarkable response to the HIV–AIDS epidemic in New

Zealand. The prostitutes' collective, which has been pivotal to the success of New Zealand's response, had been the organizer of safe sex drives among sex workers, and the members had also volunteered to help men dying of AIDS.

We gathered at my wife's house on Mt. Pleasant Road, above the pollution of the city's wood-burning fireplaces and overlooking the snow-covered Southern Alps and an estuary opening to the Pacific Ocean. The seven of us who attended the meeting included my wife and me, Anna Reed, the local solicitor, a poised young sex worker, and two transsexual women, also sex workers. We gathered over a bottle of a good Shiraz and rich Danish pastry and began to work.

The fears these women faced were much like those of any lay witnesses. The court setting was not only anxiety-provoking to them, but also antagonistic. They were frightened of difficult questions and afraid they would freeze or panic in the witness stand. Sasha, one of the transsexuals, knew from experience about the personal attacks. Hers had begun when she was held in detention and continued to the time of her trial for soliciting. The police made scathing comments about her, always referred to her by her prior male name, and sought intentionally to diminish her as a person. By the time she actually got on the stand, she already felt so worthless and demeaned that she could not think of managing to present herself as credible.

Our evening wore on, and the Danish and wine were consumed. The sex workers had brought three pages of questions they most feared. One concern was having their profession used against them during criminal trials of men who had raped them. The issue was one of consent. The cross-examination questions about the sex workers having implicitly consented were much like the questions raised with any rape victim on the witness stand. Some of the responses to implications of consent during cross-examination that I suggested included these:

"If you think for a second that this assault was in any way okay with me, you are wrong."

"Every woman, regardless of what she does for a living, finds it devastating to be raped."

"I cannot tell you too much how terrible this was for me."

"There is a huge difference between my being in control

and choosing to be sexual, in both my personal life and in my work, and having my body so violated against my will."

The other issue we worked on was the struggle for custody and visitation rights in family court. Because family courts tend to be informal, attorneys are often given great leeway in questioning the parents. Some of the questions these sex workers feared and possible answers to these questions included, "Isn't it true you have had sexual intercourse and oral sex with thousands of men, most of whom you do not even know by name?"

That question is intended to make the witness feel disreputable and ashamed, as do many questions asked of parents in custody battles. We should remember that every parent has done things he or she would prefer not to be used for custody decisions, and that the court is committed to the best interests of the child. Some answers might include the following:

- The simple push–pull: "Oh yes, it has probably been many thousands."
- The matter of fact admission: "That is correct."
- Going to the heart of the question: "If you think that my work interferes with how much I love and care for my child, you are missing how important motherhood is to me."

This question is sometimes followed by how the mother is likely to be away from the child during evenings, how the mother may have (or be prone to get) a sexually transmitted disease, and how the finding out that his or her mother is a prostitute might affect the child. Each of these questions may be answered by attending to the core issue of responsible, loving parenting.

"I consider it a basic responsibility to ensure that really good child care is there every time I leave my child to go to work, just as I hope every mother does."

"I take very seriously my responsibility to protect myself sexually. But I also know there are millions of people with really serious diseases who are wonderful parents."

"For us as sex workers it is always a tough question of what to tell our children about our work. But I believe that tough questions always come up in parenting and I surely hope that real loving and deep caring will allow my children and me to continue to love each other. I know I am committed to taking care of my children in the best way I know how."

This discussion is not about sex workers. Rather, it is about witnesses who are asked questions that address personally sensitive and socially problematic issues. For such witnesses—and each of us has the potential to be in that role—my advice is to attempt to go back to the core elements of your strength and belief in yourself. The questions during cross-examination are typically designed to diminish or discredit us. The antidote is to affirm with clarity and conviction what it is we believe and the value of who we are.

You may ask, suppose a person believes she is someone worthless who merits degradation? Courtrooms are not congenial sites for correcting such negative self-concepts. Indeed, they are toxic environments in that sense. In such cases, be aware of the negative self-assessment, but balance it with a clear, determined commitment not to let that negative piece of yourself emerge. It is easier advised than done, of course, but the resolve to do so may help.

The Maxim: Hostile attacks on one's character are best met with clear affirmations of worth and restatements of the essential issues.

26

Offensive Language

THIS STORY OF OFFENSIVE LANGUAGE was told to me by a divorce attorney.[10] In the course of a drawn-out and embittered divorce and custody dispute, a conciliation conference had been arranged and was under way. Arthur, the divorce attorney, was sitting with his client, the wife, across the table from the husband, a local well-known attorney, when the husband yelled at Arthur, "You fucking Kike!" Arthur sat stunned as a tirade ensued, with this epithet repeated several times. Arthur escorted the husband down the corridor to the judge's chambers, where the judge was available to listen to Arthur's concerns. Eight times more, now in front of the judge, the husband yelled out the same insult at Arthur, who promptly asked the judge to have the husband removed from the courthouse. For reasons unknown to Arthur, the judge declined and the conference broke up.

This particular story has a pleasing ending. The incident made its way a few weeks later into the major newspaper in this Pennsylvania city, with adverse publicity and consequences for the husband. It does raise the question of what to do if you are ever

---

[10]I have abbreviated the story considerably.

faced with a similar situation—that is, of being in a legal situation (but obviously not in court) and one of the parties insults you in terms most offensive to you. For one woman colleague of mine, the word "slut" is so offensive that she cannot tolerate it being used about any woman. For others, various racial, ethnic, or religious slurs have the capacity for being egregiously offensive.

Does it make a difference, as well, if the remarks are made by other professionals or by the parties one is evaluating? I believe so. There is a degree of emotional detachment one learns and maintains with evaluees that may not come as easily with other professionals. Four courses of action seem possible in this type of case. One choice, but not necessarily the best option, is to do what Arthur did, namely, to go immediately to the court for guidance.

A second option is to hold one's pen up pointedly, to interrupt the flow of the conversation, and visibly to write down the offending remark, noting the time, other observers, and the full statement the offender made. Why? The person who has just insulted you sees that you are recording what has been said, which leads to a shift in perceived power by itself. Indeed, it may bring out a quick apology for fear of future retribution. Further, writing it down, even if a court reporter is typing, creates an explicit paper record of the exchange for whatever possible accusation, procedures, or hearings related to it that may occur. Someone may accuse you of being biased in a report or in testimony because of this incident. With a carefully documented record, your role becomes transformed from active participant to conscientious recorder.

Confronting the speaker is a third legitimate option. I do this often when I am with people—in and out of legal settings—when they use a racial or ethnic slur. I tell the individual in careful but precise terms and with emotional neutrality, "You should know that I find the use of that word extremely offensive and I would appreciate it if you were never to use that word around me." This confrontive response is a conversation stopper.

Fourth, the options of consulting with respected colleagues and withdrawing from the case should be considered. Some situations generate such heat that few of us can handle them on our own. Good consultation can help address anger and frustration. Of course, withdrawal from the case is an altogether acceptable choice when objectivity is lost or one's integrity cannot be maintained.

Such attacks with offensive language on expert witnesses are rare, but not unheard of. Charles Patrick Ewing (personal communication, November 9, 1998) reported this situation:

> (I was) testifying for a civil plaintiff who had allegedly been brutally assaulted by the defendant. I had never met or spoken to the defendant until a break in my testimony when I passed him in the hallway outside the courtroom. He looked at me and said, "You whore!" Upon returning to the witness stand, I was cross-examined by his attorney who made a point of immediately establishing that I had never met or even spoken to the defendant. "That's not true," I replied. Astonished, the attorney asked me when I had spoken to his client. "I didn't speak to him," I said. "He saw me in the hallway a few minutes ago and called me a whore." That one made the newspapers.

The Maxim: Flagrantly offensive language never has to be met passively. Options include going to the judge, recording the statement, confronting the speaker, consulting with colleagues, withdrawing from the case, or using the information as part of one's testimony.

27

Personal Attacks

O NE OF THE MOST IMPASSIONED descriptions of personal attacks
on experts I have ever received came from Dr. Ralph Underwager who has spent 25 years in evaluations and testifying for the
defense in child abuse allegations. Dr. Underwager described the
nature of some of the abusive tactics which he has faced. As a
starting point, he observed (personal communication, June 11,
1998)[11] ". . . any expert witness must be prepared for vigorous, often vicious, personal attacks from adversaries. This is especially
true when the crime, such as child abuse, is one which has been
politicized and elicits intense emotions from all those involved."

This expert reported that he and his partner have testified
in over 350 trials and many more depositions, and have reviewed
documents in over 1,500 cases. Here are some of the experiences
and accusations he reported:

"A New Jersey prosecutor told the jury I was faking using a
cane to walk in order to appear more sympathetic."

"A Hawaii prosecutor said I had no reason to be upset at

---

[11]An alternate and critical perspective on the Underwager work and testimony may
be seen in Salter (1998).

the death of our son because he was not my biological child. At that same trial, when I extended my hand to their expert, he spit on my hand."

"Others have falsely claimed I had been an attorney, been disbarred, moved, changed my name, and became a psychologist."

He was also accused of having been expelled from the clergy; being an admitted pedophile; deliberately testifying so as to send children back to their abusers; coming to Oklahoma City to kidnap and abuse children; charging $15,000 a day; making over $1,000,000 a year; and publishing only in vanity presses.

In addition, Dr. Underwager receives death threats once or twice a year, has been picketed several times, and reports that his activities and movements are sometimes tracked carefully, and his privacy invaded in a variety of other ways. I can speak for one aspect of these personal attacks. A number of postings I have read on Internet lists accuse him of personally and professionally seeking to promote sexual relations between adults and children.

In his letter to me, Dr. Underwager offers this perspective on such attacks:

> The only way to prepare for personal attacks is to work hard at making sure every one of my opinions is supported by valid and reliable scientific research. This is, of course, what is also ethically proper for a psychologist and so should not be a hardship nor anything surprising. . . . My partner and I work very hard at being sure that we can support every opinion we express with credible and reliable quantified scientific data. In our Resource File we now have over 23,000 articles each of which we have read, evaluated, classified and entered in our computer data base.
>
> There is no reason or motivation for a psychologist to enter the forensic arena and to endure these attacks other than a commitment to the rationality of science and the conviction that such accurate scientific information is ultimately beneficial to all of us. It is best to stay away from the courtroom if this is not a central overriding value.

The Underwager example is unusual in his high visibility, the nature of his work, and the severity and personal nature of the attacks against him. Nevertheless, witnesses should be prepared for the possibility of personal attacks, especially in cases in contentious areas. Some trial attorneys routinely enter into an attacking mode of the most personal nature when they examine expert witnesses, and other attorneys resort to personal innuendo and attempts to discredit the witnesses when they have no substantive basis for cross-examination. Note that these unpleasant attacks can be levelled on personal integrity, on traits of the individual expert, and on dubious material that emerged from rumor, guesswork, or from a focus on selected aspects of the expert's career. The other side of cross-examinations, which is lucid inquiry into scientific and professional foundations of testimony, is altogether different and is a legitimate part of the trial process for which witnesses should be knowledgeably prepared.

When the attacks are ad hominum and personally intrusive, what should the expert witness do? I have four suggestions:

1. Never attack back in kind. It is not the role of the expert to exchange insults with opposing counsel. Even for witnesses whose characteristic style is to engage in outdoing others in contentious situations, the witness stand calls for setting such argumentativeness aside.
2. Maintain dignity and poise. This instruction is, of course, more easily offered than mastered, especially if one is suggested to be a fraud, an alcoholic, or a fanatic. Nevertheless, the good witness addresses the issues in a way that indicates composure and stability.
3. Use negative assertions. That is, begin your responses with statements like "No, quite to the contrary," and "That's not so at all. You have it completely wrong."
4. Do not act battered. If the personal attacks have appeared to work, witnesses look diminished on the stand. Maintaining a solid presence means avoiding the defeated look, voice quality, and body language of the battered witness.

Personal attacks in such a public arena as the witness stand are indeed difficult. Nobody likes to be attacked. However, anybody who testifies on a regular basis will eventually run into some form of personal attacks that will be allowed by the court.

The Maxim: Scholarly preparation, composure, and negative assertions are preferred responses to personal attacks.

28

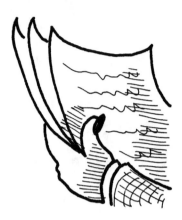

Practice Answers

SCREENWRITERS FOR FILMS AND TELEVISION master the art of compressing lengthy events into brief, pointed sequences of dialogue. Because screenplays go to the essence of conversations, they are useful for examining core relationship issues.

One episode of the courtroom drama *the practice* dealt partly with a murder charge by showing the direct and cross-examination of a psychotherapist, Dr. Gale, who had treated the murder victim. The transcript of Dr. Gale's testimony will be used in this chapter as the basis for commentary about what makes good and bad testimony. Dr. Gale was called as a defense witness and the show begins partway through the direct examination (Kelley, 1997). The defense attorney is Bobby Donnell.

> Bobby Donnell: You treated the victim for how long, Dr. Gale?
>
> Dr. Gale: Just under six years.
>
> Bobby Donnell: And during the course of your therapy sessions with Mr. Adler, did he ever talk about my client?
>
> Dr. Gale: Occasionally
>
> Bobby Donnell: Do you remember what he said about her?
>
> Dr. Gale: Not really. He just mentioned she was a neighbor

who lived on the same apartment floor and that he and
his wife would frequently visit with her.

Bobby Donnell: Okay. You've heard the prosecutor's suggestion that the victim was perhaps having a sexual affair
with my client?

Dr. Gale: I've heard the suggestion, yes.

Bobby Donnell: Do you have a response?

Dr. Gale: My response would be that it's ridiculous. I knew
almost every detail of Robert Adler's life. There was no
such affair.

[*The better answer to this question would be "My response would
be that it is unlikely that there was such an affair." Gale's response
is a substantial overstatement, phrased in absolutist terms.*]

Bobby Donnell: Well, is it possible that he would have kept
this from you?

Dr. Gale: Frankly, No. Bob Adler would pour out his deepest
intimacies in my office, the man gave me progress reports
on his hemorrhoids. If he were having an affair with
somebody, I surely would have known about it.

[*The use of the word "frankly" is not necessary. No hint has been
offered that Dr. Gale is being anything but frank. Furthermore,
whenever witnesses respond with "to be honest with you" or
"frankly," many listeners assume that what is about to be said may
be untruthful. The phrase that is the key element of the question is
"is it possible?" Witnesses should think through their replies with
care before denying that some event or psychological process is possible. I would never assume that a therapy client is totally disclosing
with me. In Gale's position, I might answer, "Although it is possible,
it is highly unlikely, based on my knowledge of Bob Adler."*]

Bobby Donnell: On this you're positive?

Dr. Gale: Very: the only relationship he had with your client
was that of a neighborly friendship.

Bobby Donnell: Thank you, Dr. Gale.

Cross-Examination by Helen Gamble, the prosecuting attorney

113

Helen Gamble: What were you treating Mr. Adler for?
Dr. Gale: Very mild depression.

[Dr. Gale has used the word "very" twice in two sentences. That repetition diminishes the power of his statements. Avoid empty modifiers like "very" that add little to the meaning of a sentence.]

Ms. Gamble: Do you remember how he first came to you? Anybody refer him?
Dr. Gale: Yes.

[Two questions are asked here. Attentive witnesses may choose to note the two questions by stating "You have asked me two questions." A reasonable alternative is to reply "Yes, I do remember how he first came to me and, yes, somebody did refer him." This reply empowers the witness more than the simple "yes" reply.]

Ms. Gamble: Do you remember who?
Dr. Gale: His wife, Mary.
Ms. Gamble: And how did Mary Adler know of you?
Dr. Gale: She's been my patient for nine years.
Ms. Gamble: I see, so you would have kind of a trusting relationship with Mary Adler then?
Dr. Gale: Yes.
Ms. Gamble: In fact, nine years, I'd imagine you two have built up quite a trust.
Dr. Gale: We have.

[The introduction of the word "trust" here is used as if both questioner and witness know what it means in this context. Are they talking about the trust by the therapist? The client? About trust in the emotional safety of the therapy situation? The questioner skillfully moved from using the phrase "kind of a trusting relationship" to the catch-all term "trust." Dr. Gale would have been well-off describing what kind of trust was present, and not present, too.]

Ms. Gamble: And *given* that trust, if you knew somebody to be betraying Mary Adler, wouldn't you feel some sort of obligation to tell her?

Dr. Gale: I *didn't* know of any . . . [*word "betrayal" cut off*]

[*He didn't hear the question about the implied obligation to tell. Instead, he inappropriately challenged the assumption underlying the question. In these circumstances, some judges would order a witness to answer the question.*]

Ms. Gamble: Please listen to my question, Sir. If you knew of someone to be betraying Mary Adler, a client you'd established a nine year trust with, would you tell her?

Dr. Gale: It's not so easy. If I learned it from another client, there would be tremendous conflicts of interest, counsel.

[*What is he talking about? If he learned somehow of this affair, why would he feel any obligation to tell her? The commonsense reply about* boundaries *evaded him, presumably under the pressure of the questioning.*]

Ms. Gamble: You're a very good witness.

Bobby Donnell: Objection.

Judge: Sustained. Strike that.

Ms. Gamble: It's not so easy, you say. So, there would be some pull on you to tell her, wouldn't there? I mean Mary Adler trusts you. If you were to find out she was being betrayed, there would be some pull on you to tell, whether you would end up doing it or not, Right?

Dr. Gale: Obviously.

[*The question is posed in such a way that Dr. Gale agrees too quickly. The question is asked twice, and rephrased in such a manner to elicit agreement. Dr. Gale falls for it. This question of whether there is a pull to tell is not necessarily obvious. In the same situation, I might answer, "Not necessarily."*]

Ms. Gamble: Obviously. And this might be obvious to Robert Adler too, wouldn't it?

Dr. Gale: Perhaps.

Ms. Gamble: Perhaps. So couldn't it be Robert Adler thought

it best not to tell you he was sleeping with Victoria Keenan?

Bobby Donnell: Objection.

Judge: Overruled.

Ms. Gamble: Isn't it at least *possible* given your conflicts of interest, your fiduciary relationship with his wife, that Robert Adler chose not to tell you he was committing adultery with that woman?

Dr. Gale: I don't think that was the case.

[*Again, the question was not heard. The question was about possibility, not actuality.*]

Ms. Gamble: Is it your testimony that such a scenario is impossible, Doctor?

Dr. Gale: No. I am not saying it's impossible.

Ms. Gamble: Thank you, Doctor. The truth isn't so painful after all. Is it?

[*That last comment is one of the loaded, gratuitous insults that attorneys occasionally make, and that commonly elicits an objection. If there were a chance to reply, the annoyed witness might well state that, no, only these kinds of half-truths are painful.*]

(later that night in Bobby Donnell's office)

Bobby Donnell: This is why I hate psychiatric experts. In the end they always wobble.

Eugene Young, Second defense attorney: It's not exactly a black and white science.

[*To the contrary, psychiatric experts do not always wobble. It depends on the experts, attorneys, questions, and issues. Giving the court what it is entitled to is not wobbling. Finally, all sciences have some element of subjectivity. No field of science is fully black or white.*]

The Maxim: Maintaining integrity on the stand calls for careful listening, avoidance of anticipatory answers, and staying faithful to your findings and knowledge.

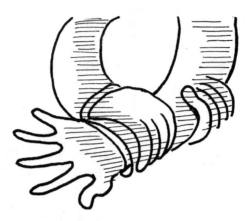

29

Pulling and the Push-Pull

SOME OF THE SIMPLEST IDEAS in theory are difficult to master in practice: regular flossing after meals, the nature of Zen riddles, the unicycle, and when to buy a new computer. Of course, some difficult ideas are also hard to master, like the writings of Jacques Derrida (e.g., Derrida, 1988) and algebraic topology (Smith, 1997). One of the simple ideas about testifying that has repeatedly demanded my attention has been the push–pull. The "push" in the push–pull is an aggressive question that an attorney has designed to make witnesses feel deficient. The pull in the push–pull is the enthusiastic endorsement of the pushy but accurate implication of the question. The "pull" response always moves in the same conceptual direction as the question. Here are some characteristic pushes, drawn from many possibilities:

- You are not perfect, are you Doctor?
- Psychological knowledge is not infallible, is it?
- Psychology is art as much as science, isn't it?
- Don't you sometimes make mistakes without knowing it?
- Was your examination complete and perfect in every way?
- Isn't it true that psychology still has a long way to go as a profession?

- Isn't there a great deal of disagreement in your field about whether diagnoses are objective and scientific?
- Have you ever made simple addition mistakes in scoring tests?
- Have you read the articles related to the issues in this case that have been published in scholarly journals this year?
- If you had unlimited time, aren't there things you would have done in this case that you did not do?
- Do the tests you used meet the American Psychological Association *Essential* criteria in the APA Standards for Psychological and Educational Tests?

When I wrote earlier about how to handle these kinds of questions (Brodsky, 1991), the answer was presented as a simple one: go in the same direction as the questioner. Do not shrink back or attack defensively, and do not overexplain. Do not deny that you make errors. Do not assert that you would have performed the exact same procedures if you had unlimited time. All of these responses are defensive in nature and diminish the power of the response and the credibility of the witness. The questions deserve an honest response of inadequacies. However, the manner in which personal and professional inadequacies are acknowledged influences the witnesses' credibility and effectiveness.

The push–pull consists of pulling in the same direction the attorney pushes, so that the witness gains ownership of the exchange.

Take the opening question in the above list:

"You are not perfect, are you, Doctor?"

A good push–pull agrees and then emphasizes the agreement, so that the reply is a sign of mastery rather than grudging admission of imperfection. A good answer is "Most certainly, no, I would never for a second portray myself nor anyone else I have ever met in my whole life as perfect!" (The implied but unstated commentary in this kind of reply to the attorney is "Of course not, you buffoon.")

Let us go again to one of the opening questions:

"Isn't there a great deal of disagreement in your field about whether diagnoses are objective and scientific?"

The overly qualified, potentially ineffectual response is

"Well, those of us who test and have experience in the field are confident about the results," or "Diagnosis has gotten better with the use of norms and with standardized assessment methods for the *DSM-IV* diagnoses.

The push–pull stays exactly with the topic, with momentum that shifts ownership to the witness. One example of this is "There is a HUGE amount of disagreement in the field about the objectivity and scientific nature of diagnoses."

Once the attorneys hear this kind of reply, they are going to be tip-toe cautious about pursuing it further because they have heard the witness's comfort and apparent knowledge. The wise attorney might slip away with a hint of success in a condescending "Thank you for that honest admission" and move to another topic. Many attorneys get greedy and unwisely seek to capitalize on this moment and pursue it further by asking questions such as "So, Doctor, you agree that reasonable scientific doubts exist about whether your diagnosis is scientific and objective?"

The follow-up response might well be "No. Quite to the contrary. Despite the disagreement about the details of diagnosis, there are compelling professional, scientific, and behavioral reasons to conclude that the plaintiff has a severe and incapacitating thought disorder."

In every workshop on expert testimony, I teach the push–pull as a mechanism to deal with statements designed to make witnesses feel guilty and stupid. I continue to be startled by how difficult it is for so many professionals to acknowledge weaknesses of these sorts. Instead of simple admissions or push–pulls, they make a variety of other efforts to cope. What, in fact, they do is:

- They equivocate.
- They dither.
- They babble on in seemingly endless verbiage.
- They act slyly.
- They act vain.

This is the way people often respond when they are under fire. It takes practice to master the push–pull. Largely because strong agreement with a pushy question is counter-intuitive, witnesses often avoid both simple admissions of truthful answers as well as forget to "pull" when the attorneys "push." For practice, I suggest writing a list of five genuine weaknesses in your background, in your specialty work, or in your typical evaluations. Choose weaknesses that make you cringe. Then have a colleague or friend ask questions on each topic in an insistent manner. If you can "pull" energetically and nonapologetically with each "push," then you will have gone a long way toward being prepared for such questions on the stand.

The Maxim: Pulling in a push–pull exchange is an art that requires nondefensive responding and meaningful practice.

30

Real and Apparent Ambiguities[12]

ONE IMPORTANT FORENSIC ISSUE is how to account for differences in expert opinions. Why will two trained professionals look at an individual and arrive at markedly opposing opinions? This question sometimes arises in depositions or court testimony when attorneys suggest that the opinions of experts retained by opposing counsel are meaninglessness. Cross-examination or deposition questions like the following ones address this issue:

"Do you believe you are better educated than Dr. White?"

"Didn't you use the same methodology as Dr. White?"

"Is there any scientific reason to believe your opinions are more correct than those of Dr. White?"

One response to these queries goes like this: "I cannot speak for anybody else and how they reached their conclusions. I can only offer my conclusions and my opinions, and I hope they will be of assistance to the court." In other instances, witnesses will describe in some detail the (presumably superior) methodology or training they bring to the task, but that response carries the risk of

---

[12]The title for this chapter was taken from the book title *Real and Apparent Ambiguities* by Barry Levy (1997).

the expert being seen as self-aggrandizing. Furthermore, proving that one's training, methodology, or conclusions are superior and correct is a difficult task in the social and behavioral sciences.

Such responses do not always answer the core question of why qualified experts reach different conclusions. The two answers I hear at workshops are that many opposing experts provide "bought" opinions, and testify exclusively for one side, or that opposing experts are driven by passion for a cause. I know some of these purported bought experts who do have opinions that differ from some of their colleagues, but I am not convinced their opinions are bought. Fierce personal convictions can also overwhelm objectivity, but this is uncommon.

For both categories, the *perceived* number of compromised experts is vastly larger than what is probably the *true* number. If the cause of discrepancies between experts is not compromised by money or convictions, what then are the causes?

The causes of differences in expert opinions come about from two sources: first, real or genuine ambiguities, and, second, perceived ambiguities. As a starting point, let us define ambiguity to mean that more than one interpretation of a phenomenon, behavior, or event is possible. This definition allows the locus of differential interpretations to be in the event as well as in the interpreter. There are also two less common definitions of ambiguity: being uncertain or unclear (Kooij, 1971); and being both true and false at the same time (Saarinen, 1981).

Given these definitions, let us now consider "real" ambiguities in the information on which mental health experts depend. First is the nature of the clinical interview with its variable choice and phrasing of questions, tone of voice in questions and answers, relative weighting or emphasis on the different replies, and the nature of follow-up inquiries. In other words, ambiguity lies within normal professional discretion.

Real ambiguities in methodology also arise in part from real differences in training and knowledge. Some assessors are trained more in interviewing techniques, whereas others are trained more in test interpretation. Still others have special expertise in detecting malingering and may find malingering in content that most assessors would not.

Apparent ambiguities in assessments may include variable

interpretations of content within employment records, medical histories, military service information, arrest and conviction data, family information, and so on. Although various evaluators might make something different (thus, apparent ambiguity) of histories of lower back pain or panic attacks, the data themselves may be reasonably clear.

The implication for reconciling differences in opinions of experts is to look at the least ambiguous, task-relevant data. The more such common information is available, the greater opportunities will exist for understanding the points of departure between experts in interpretations and conclusions.

The labelling of opposing experts as bought or wearing blinders is an unbecoming and unproductive process. It seems to demean the accuser and rarely seems to promote healthy discourse about the reasons for such differences. It is more useful to pursue common grounds for our work, and to recognize the reasons that differences of opinion may come from the same events.

The Maxim: Real ambiguities exist in understanding and interpreting behaviors of defendants and litigants. Opposing experts who disagree with you are not necessarily corrupt, dim, or myopic.

31

Reconstructing Your Testimony

> As a trial lawyer, you do not control the meaning of what you say. The speaker's intent has only the vaguest correlation with the juror's interpretation, as every lawyer learns who speaks to the jurors after a trial. (Steven Lubet, 1998, p. 2)

When Steven Lubet of the Northwestern University Law School made these comments, he was introducing his talk about alternative interpretations of Atticus Finch and the alleged rape in *To Kill a Mockingbird* (Lee, 1960). Titling his talk "Reconstructing Atticus Finch," Lubet argued that the complaint by Mayella Ewell of the rape was attacked by Atticus in part because of her low social class. Furthermore, Atticus Finch was presented in the narrative by his 9-year-old daughter Scout as a paragon of virtue and truth, when an equally compelling interpretation was that he was "just another working lawyer playing out his narrow, determined role" (Lubet, 1998, p. 2). Lubet noted that Atticus used the demeaning "She wanted it" form of the "consent" defense. "Atticus tortured Mayella. He held her up as a sexual aggressor at a time when such conduct was absolutely dishonorable and disgraceful" (p. 13). Lubet went on to say that the unnoticed flaws in Harper Lee's anti-racism storytelling were her portrayals of gender and class bias.

This reconsideration of Atticus Finch requires a radical re-thinking of a major fictional hero. In a related sense, I suggest that many of us who testify have unknowingly constructed personal fictions of how we are heard and that these constructions call for a serious rethinking. We often believe that we are persuasive, lucid, and coherent when we are not. And vice versa. Our language and vocabulary usage, the stereotyped perceptions of professionals and experts, and excessive attention by jurors to minor statements or behaviors are just part of what lead to impressions very different from those we infer. It is only now and then that an opportunity arises to learn about these differences.

One such difference in the interpretation of spoken language occurred when I was a Visiting Fellow at the National Institute of Mental Health And Neuro Sciences (NIMHANS) in Bangalore, India. NIMHANS used to be exclusively a psychiatric hospital and was known to locals as The Mental Hospital. One day I asked an English-speaking driver of an autoshaw, a motorized rickshaw, to take me to the mental hospital. He asked with puzzlement where I wanted to go, and I repeated "mental hospital."

"Mental hospital?" he asked again.

"Yes. Mental hospital," I replied.

Still confused, he repeated, "Mental hospital?"

A passing businessman offered to help. I explained to him that was I was trying to go to the mental hospital and the driver did not understand me. In what seemed to be the exact same pronunciation and inflection, he said to the driver, "Mental hospital."

The driver lit up. "Oh! Mental hospital!" he exclaimed with delight and understanding, and took me there.

This story indicates how I believed I was communicating in a way that would be fully understood by both the driver and the businessman. Yet major differences existed between what I thought I was saying and what was received and interpreted by the driver. Now as then, I do not know what accounted for this miscommunication.

So it goes in court testimony. We believe we are making ourselves understood. The audience is paying attention to us, sometimes nodding, and seeming to understand what we say. Our confidence in our clarity is belied by the results: misunderstandings that only become apparent to us at a later time when it is too late to change the impressions we have created.

An illustrative story is told by Charles Patrick Ewing (personal communication, November 8, 1998) of one case in which he testified:

> I had testified on the complicated psychophysiological arousal effects on a murder defendant who had been attacked and fought with another man just an hour before killing a third party in what appeared to be self-defense. After explaining the psychophysiology of arousal, I gave the jurors what I thought was a clever analogy. I suggested considering how much liquid would be required to overflow an empty glass (someone in a normal nonaroused state) versus how much less it would take to overflow a glass already half full (someone in an emotionally aroused state). After the jury acquitted the defendant (a Black man who had stabbed one of several white men who surrounded him an hour after the initial fight), defense counsel spoke to the jurors, several of whom asked "What the hell was all that about the glass of water?" From what they said, it appears that most of my testimony went completely over their heads, and my efforts to simplify it were unappreciated.

How do we find out how well we have been understood by the triers of fact? There are several paths, none of which is altogether satisfactory, but which are listed here in order of increasing desirability.

- Ask the attorney who has retained you. However, attorneys tend not to criticize experts they have retained, and once the testimony is over, become much less invested in what you have said and how it has been received. The standard response is reassurance. Only when the attorneys are unusually responsive is there a reasonable chance of getting useful feedback from this inquiry.
- Ask a nonprofessional friend or significant other to observe. The friend should take notes. The debriefing should probably take the form of asking the friend to paraphrase your state-

ments in his or her own words. The payoffs from this approach are sometimes satisfactory and worthwhile.

- Ask the jurors yourself. Once the case is concluded, there usually is no prohibition against contact between witnesses and the jurors. However, jurors may be reluctant to say anything negative or, indeed, anything at all. I recently called some jurors to ask some relatively impersonal questions about one aspect of a trial. One of the jurors was unequivocal; she preferred not to talk about it with me or anyone else. Another juror was slightly more forthcoming. He was willing to talk but he remembered little about any of the issues or witnesses' testimony in the case.

- Contract with a jury consultation and survey group. These professionals are accustomed to approaching jurors, they can help formulate questions that will get at the essential issues that matter to you, and they can be dispassionate in their tasks. Although some expense is involved in this option, it also has the opportunity for the fullest feedback. Attorneys who have lost cases they expected to win sometimes contract with firms to survey jurors. The quality of obtained information is still dependent on jurors' willingness to talk, but jurors are more willing to talk with parties who are independent of the case.

We don't like to think of Atticus Finch as just another lawyer, because we have such a long history of thinking of him as an archetype of moral integrity. Similarly, because we have such long histories of habituation to and valuing of our own professional thoughts, we don't like to think of ourselves as just people who may be misunderstood. When we learn that we are not communicating well, changing our long-established habits of communication is far from automatic. Prochaska and Norcross (1994) see change in psychotherapy as beginning with precontemplation of change and then contemplation of change, well before actual behavior and emotional changes take place. Directed feedback about our court testimony probably puts us in a position of precontemplation, ready to start thinking about changes in our ways of testifying. The work of continuing to get feedback on language, behaviors, and presentation of self is a major and demanding goal.

The Maxim: Assumptions about what and how you are communicating on the stand need to be checked and rechecked.

32

Shifts in Testifying and Consulting Expertise

T HESE NEXT TWO CASES came up side by side. In the first, a complex civil case, I had worked on an evaluation of medical and psychological records and numerous depositions over a period of some years. Because of the continuing series of delays, extended discovery, repeated motions from both sides for summary judgments, and then my own affidavits and depositions, I had spoken by telephone about 50 times with the attorney who retained me and spoken in person about a dozen times. We had not become friends, but he and I had become friendly as we explored the developing nature of this case and my contribution as an evaluating expert. We were on a first name basis most of the time (except in any correspondence or hearings) and he asked sophisticated and intelligent questions about the nature of my assessment and the meaning of my results. We developed a mutual respect and a warm rapport over this extended period of time.

The various motions for summary judgments were not granted, the time extensions to discovery eventually ran out, the judge's insistent demands for a settlement could not be worked out, and the trial date was suddenly upon us. Knowing that I also work as a trial consultant and in jury selection, the attorney informed me "The jury composition is going to determine whether we win or lose."

"Uh-huh," I replied, in my best clinical manner, suspecting what was going to come next.

"The venire doesn't look good, and I am struggling," he said. "This trial is going to be tough. What do you think we should look for in jurors? And what kinds of people do we need to strike?"

"I don't think I can be of help. Sorry. Wish I could," I answered.

"Well," he persisted, "do you have suggestions for questions I might use in the voir dire?"

"If I were not an expert witness in the trial, I would be happy to work on the jury selection. Because I will testify as an expert, it would be a conflict of interest for me. I cannot testify as an impartial expert on what I found, and at the same time help you pick a jury. I would then be on your side as an advocate and I can't do that."

"Oh. Okay," the attorney responded. "I hope you are not offended."

When it came to my testimony, I did make suggestions about the questions this attorney should ask me to ensure that my findings were presented in an organized and clear way. Furthermore, I did guide the attorney on how to construct courtroom charts that showed the sequence of records, events, and depositions I had evaluated, so that I might refer to them as I testified. These suggestions all related to my own findings and had to do with how I would be examined on direct and my being effective in communicating my findings. These latter comments seemed altogether fitting to me. If I had agreed earlier to aid in the jury selection, that act would have made me part of the attorney's team, and I would have been compromised as an independent and objective expert.

At approximately the same time as these events were unfolding, a criminal case in which I had been engaged as an expert was finally coming to trial. I had been retained by the court-appointed counsel for a man accused of murder. Unlike the more conventional mental responsibility or competency assessments of accused criminals, this second case had called for an exploration of the nature of the referral question. The defendant had been living with a woman who claimed to be pregnant but who had had a hysterectomy years earlier. While the defendant was at work, the woman allegedly shot a genuinely pregnant acquaintance in the head and then cut the full term child from the victim, claiming it as her own. Either knowingly or not, the defendant helped dispose of a sealed barrel in which the victim's corpse had been placed.

One essential issue that would be contested in court was whether the defendant had truly been fooled by his girlfriend's claim that she was pregnant. If he had been, then her showing up with a new baby would be consistent with the rest of his statement. With the *a priori* understanding that I could not testify about whether he actually knew she was pregnant or not, we proceeded. Part of my evaluation included an intellectual and personality assessment using a WAIS, an MMPI, a TAT, and an administration of the Gudjonsson Suggestibility Scale-2. The Gudjonsson Scale requires participants to recall a story they were told an hour earlier. After natural recall is recorded, the participants are told they did badly in recall, and a new measure is obtained of how influenced participants are by the test administrator's comments. On this task the defendant scored close to the maximum level of suggestibility. Compelling results clearly in hand, I was ready to go to court with my findings.

One week before the trial, the defendant's attorneys met with me and asked if I would serve as a jury consultant. It took an hour to explore what they had in mind, and I agreed to work as a trial consultant instead of as a testifying expert. Three principles that have broader application, and that distinguished this case from the one discussed above, emerged from my participation in this discussion and the decision to consult.

First, if one is going to be an expert witness, one cannot be a jury consultant. Much like the case noted earlier, it would represent a conflict of roles.

Second, the attorneys need to be absolutely certain of their preferences, because consulting experts must withdraw from any objective, evaluative role with the defendant. In my case the attorneys asserted that their preference was to have me be a jury consultant because they had many fact witnesses who would address the suggestibility and pregnancy issues.

Third, this new course of action is a one-way street. Once experts start working in any meaningful way as a jury consultant, they can not and should not serve as expert witnesses. It is important in the ethics of forensic experts that this one-way street works only to change their role from evaluating expert to trial consultant, that is, from impartiality to advocacy in the sense of planning and assisting in the jury selection, case conceptualization, and trial strategy. It is unethical to move from jury or trial consultant to evaluating expert. Once committed to an advocacy role, the alliance with the attorneys includes a commitment to help win the case. That starting point makes it impossible to become an impartial expert with one's concurrent commitment to help the court.

The Maxim: Evaluating experts can legitimately give up their roles as expert witnesses to become jury or trial consultants, but should never assume both roles, or shift from jury or trial consultants to becoming testifying experts.

33

Silent Treatments

I N A PLACE SO FULL OF WORDS, it is sometimes surprising how many silences, both low grade and high grade, settle over courtrooms. Low grade silences are characterized by various whisperings, rustling about in seats, shuffling of papers by attorneys, clerks, or witnesses, and the breaks in proceedings when jurors or witnesses enter or leave. They are not true silences—indeed, there is no such thing as true silence in the courtroom because there are always noises of heating or air conditioning blowers, ambient sounds from outside the building, and other noises that are noticed only when there is a reason to attend to them.

High grade silences are the dead-quiet moments during which almost all intentional movement and talk is stopped, usually by a sharp break in the flow of events. The judge enters the room, often accompanied by the command to "all rise," and a high grade brief silence is enforced. For me, the most interesting high grade silences occur during crucial points in the examination of witnesses. These high grade silences work in both directions: attorneys to witnesses and witnesses to attorneys.

Let's take attorneys to witnesses first. Harold Bursztajn and Archie Brodsky (1998) observe that the silent treatment by attorneys in Zen thinking is called "The question of no question," which means a question is clearly asked or implied by a high grade silence. Bursztajn and Brodsky describe it this way, "You answer one question, and the attorney says nothing." That is, the attorney waits and by waiting indicates that your reply is incomplete or deficient. The solution is described as "You can respond by looking with the jury at the attorney, or ask, 'Is there some other way I can help you?'" (Bursztajn and Brodsky, 1998, p. 277).

What makes this situation interesting is the implicit communication of a negative judgment by the attorney. The silence that follows your reply can be unnerving for witnesses who automatically look to some form of approval from opposing counsel. It is a more elegant move for the attorney than the cliched comment–question of "Surely you are not trying to tell this court that such a short evaluation can lead unerringly to such a sweeping conclusion?"

I like the idea of peacefully waiting out an attorney who gives me the silent treatment. After all, the attorneys ask questions; the witnesses answer them. If the attorney needs more information, it is up to her or him to seek it. Suppose the attorney then asks if your answer is the only response you will make?

I suggest answering with a pleasant, comfortable "yes." A more narrative answer could be "that is exactly what I have to say about that issue."

Once the silence is recognized as a trick to unsettle you, good responses come more readily. Within the narrow constraints of this little exchange, the attorney will win if you are anxious or yield to the silent treatment; you are effective if you are unperturbed and at ease with your reply.

As a footnote to this discussion, let us observe that sometimes attorneys fall silent during direct examination. I try not to let the silences unsettle me.

Under those circumstances, I try to clear my mind and allow additional useful comments to surface. Sometimes they do. My friends who believe avidly in psychic powers attribute such thoughts surfacing to be the product of psychic transmissions, much as they attribute the availability of good parking places to visualizations that a parking spot will be there. I much prefer to think of it as the result of good preparation and good memory.

So far we have addressed the problem of attorneys who

engage in what I have termed the "silent treatment." An equal opportunity exists for witnesses to use silence. The nonverbal communication literature has addressed the nature of silences in interpersonal relationships. In their thoughtful consideration of silences in human interactions, Malandro, Barker, and Barker (1989) pointed out these functions (the comments in italics that follow each function, however, are my own observations):

- Silences are not the opposite of speech, but rather the environment surrounding spoken language. *Witnesses have partial control of how much silence is wrapped around their testimony.*
- Silences serve the function of contrast or emphasis of spoken language. *In contrast to the tendencies to give rushed replies or quick answers elicited by the pace or intensity of the question, brief silence allows the response to be measured and confident.*
- Lengthy silences can be attention-grabbing. *Some witnesses are not comfortable with silences in any form and seek to fill what they perceive as empty space with words and, if alone, with music or other entertainment. A silence makes a statement, in the sense of making an impact. Effective witnesses know what kind of impact they seek.*
- Silence helps you put thoughts into words and to experience a greater awareness of yourself and the courtroom. *I encourage you to practice thinking quietly for one full breath after the question is posed so you will have time to consider how to answer effectively and well.*
- Silence is a central part of turn-yielding behaviors and is part of turn-requesting in conversations as well. *Sometimes cross-examining attorneys will pause after a statement or after a partially formulated question, waiting for a reply. If no clear question has been asked (and no objection is made), I sit and wait. If no elaboration is forthcoming, I then say "I'm sorry. I may have missed something. Did you actually ask me a question?" At times when the attorney asks an offensive or foolish question, I may pause and look puzzled so that I communicate just how inappropriate the question is.*

The Maxim: Silence becomes us when we are not intimidated by it in cross-examination and can use it comfortably toward our own effective testimony.

34

Sleight of Hand

IN SOME DIRECT AND CROSS-EXAMINATIONS, and especially in depositions, questions are asked that make little sense to the witnesses. The questioning may be about some aspect of professional practice, or they may be about a continuing controversy, such as repressed memories of child abuse in cases that have nothing to do with repression, memory, or child abuse. The questions may also be about items in licensing examinations, about international differences in training of health professionals, or about whether John Gray or Andrea Dworkin or perhaps Nancy Friday were correct in their assertions about people's motives and behaviors. This latter line of questions is the one we will examine as illustrative of the genre; it always builds on the writings of a person who is known to both the general and professional public, and about whom the witness is presumed to be knowledgeable.

These questions are most likely to appear in depositions because the court is not in session to control the substantive flow of relevant testimony. Such questions are sometimes allowed in court when the examining attorney can provide a tenuous link to the key issues or evidence, or when the retaining attorney does not object on grounds of relevance. For example, if the case is a custody dispute, the attorney may ask if you believe that men are from Mars and women are from Venus. If there is reasonable information that a defendant in a sexual harassment case reads explicit sexual magazines at work, you might be asked to describe and discuss the Dworkin position of how pornography causes sexual abuses. If women's sexuality is at issue, you might be asked if you accept Nancy Friday's assumptions about the normal high incidence of women's sexual fantasies of rape.

To be vulnerable to this line of inquiry, the expert witness must have some knowledge of the writings of popular psychologists or other well-known social commentators. Consider it a cardinal rule that you do not discuss any writings that you have not read, and, indeed, read carefully and well. It is remarkable how many experts discuss popular writers whose views they know only from *USA Today, Newsweek,* or from appearances by the authors on television talk shows. By itself, this do-not-discuss-if-you-do-not-really-know rule will remove you from many troubling situations in depositions.

Attorneys pursue such questions for three reasons. First, they draw on what they know. Unless the case is unusually important, or unless the attorneys are somewhat scholarly to begin with, they tend not to go to substantive scientific knowledge. They ask about content that is common knowledge through the print or electronic media, or that they have personally read. They ask about John Gray because they have read Gray, have read about Gray, or have attended a talk by Gray.

A second reason for such inquiries is that the attorneys are engaged in a process rather than content mode. They ask a variety of questions in a conversational mode to gauge how well the expert will relate to a jury, as well, of course, to assess the potency of the plaintiff's case for purposes of settlement.

The third reason for such inquiries is what I have come to think of as a sleight of hand, a technique used by illusionists and magicians. The essence of sleight of hand is distraction. The audience looks at the attention-demanding gesture or attends to the dramatic and flamboyant sweeps of hands or cloths or capes, while the essential work of the illusion goes unnoticed.

Like most professionals who work with legal matters, I have sat through such questioning during depositions. My reaction is a certain degree of feeling intrigued by the gambit. In the stretch of time between the attorneys' questions and my answers, I think a little about where they are going with these questions, a little about how much they actually know about the subject, and a great deal about how much I actually know about the subject.

Declining the gambit is easy. Sometimes simply declining to answer sleight of hand questions works by just saying you don't know anything about John Gray. Sometimes an expanded answer is in order, such as explaining that you have no professional or scientific knowledge about John Gray (which, likely, will be the truth). Persistent attorneys, again especially in depositions, will ask how widely read is Gray (or Joyce Brothers or the latest fad figure in pop psychology). At this point, a clarification of the limits of one's competence may be in order, with a reply such as "If you need an estimate of the circulation of their books, you will have to look to an expert in book distribution and sales and library activity. These issues are outside my areas of practice and knowledge."

In magic shows, the sleight of hand depends on deceiving the audience through misdirection. Although skilled illusions may be difficult to detect, alert observers may spot the essential move or deception. With the equivalent of sleight of hand in attorneys' questions, the same principle applies. One has to avoid being entranced by the gesture to be successful in negotiating sleight of hand traps.

The Maxim: Witnesses are not obliged to answer all questions that appear to be related to their fields. Instead, witnesses need to attend to the direct applicability of the question and the extent to which the substance truly falls within their expertise.

35

Social Construction of
Illnesses and Disorders

S OMETIMES THE MOST CHALLENGING questions on cross-examination
come from attorneys who have been educated in other disciplines or who have a good breadth of knowledge outside the law.
When one runs into such knowledgeable attorneys, it is not just
defense of one's findings and credentials that is at issue, but also
defense of basic assumptions in one's profession.

A good example is the assumption that diagnostic clinical
entities are real, or at least as real as quarks, gigabytes, and topo-
graphic maps. The alternative assumption that may be pursued during questioning is that these constructs are no more or less real
today than were demons, Greek gods, and the Loch Ness monster
to people of other times and places.

The constructs are real in part because we agree they are
real. One well-established area of social science theory has argued
that some of our most treasured diagnostic entities are socially constructed rather than strictly factual categories that we should take
at face value. Influences on this construction may include the media
and the zeitgeist, and once so manufactured, evidence is repeatedly
found to support the constructs. Two examples particularly relevant

to litigation and court testimony are Posttraumatic Stress Disorder (PTSD) and dangerousness. Let us focus first on PTSD.

Sociologist Jerry Lee Lembcke (1997) has concluded that the diagnosis of Posttraumatic Stress Disorder for Vietnam veterans was largely a construct of the media and the government, for very different reasons. He wrote "I argue that we need to understand PTSD as much as a cultural and political category as a mental health category and that the content of PTSD—alienation, survivor guilt, and flashbacks—were derived from popular culture" (Lembcke, 1997, pp. 2–3). He acknowledges that there were lingering effects of the Vietnam war experience and that psychiatrists did play a role in establishing the PTSD diagnosis, but Lembcke goes on to make these five arguments:

1. Antiwar Vietnam veterans were a major embarrassment to the Nixon administration in 1971 and 1972 because of the almost unprecedented turning of veterans against the regime that sent them to war. After other efforts to dismiss their protests failed, the administration solution came from what may be called a discourse of disability. That is, the Nixon administration argued that veterans' protests were signs of how mentally incapacitated the veterans had been by the trauma of the war.

2. The so-called Post-Vietnam Syndrome was manufactured by an extraordinarily powerful, well-timed, and nationally accepted portrayal of eight individual veterans in the *New York Times* in August, 1972, at the same time that thousands of Vietnam vets protested at the Republican Party National Convention.

3. The PTSD concept of widespread alienation among Vietnam veterans was contradicted by research data indicating that 94% of studied veterans were welcomed home in warm and friendly ways. Lembcke observed that ". . . alienation was incorporated to the Vietnam veteran literature from the early 70s academic literature on youth culture and campus radicalism" (p. 21).

4. The concept of survivor guilt was imported from survivors of Hiroshima, with psychiatrist Robert Jay Lifton serving as the key conceptualizer in testimony to Congress and public-

ity to the nation. In fact, 85% of the GIs in Vietnam did not see combat and few of the other GIs saw sustained combat. According to Lembcke, the portrayal of terrorized helplessness seemed unsupported by facts.

5. Battle flashbacks were metaphors borrowed from the cinema. "Film makers virtually created the definition of flashback as a trauma induced, psychological phenomenon" (pp. 30–31).

Contributing to these specific PTSD concerns is a controversial body of literature that challenges the scientific foundations of the DSM itself. For example, Kirk and Kutchens (1992) have argued that the DSM diagnoses serve psychiatry and the mental health enterprise more than they aid patients, and, further, that the reliability data purported to support the DSM categories are themselves highly suspect. (Note: I will not take the space to present the counterarguments for PTSD as a scientific and useful construct, because the prevailing view is known and accepted by health professionals, including me.)

Consider these questions that possibly could be asked by an attorney who has read the Lembcke view of PTSD:

Q: Doctor, who first developed this understanding about a disorder called PTSD?

Q: Where did the concept of flashbacks come from?

Q: How is the experience of war veterans similar and dissimilar to those of rape victims?

Q: How much is a re-experiencing of a trauma like a drug flashback? How is it different?

Q: How is re-experiencing of a trauma like a flashback to an earlier time or event in a movie? How is it different?

Q: How many different kinds of PTSD are there? How much do they vary with the kind of trauma?

Q: Can one be exposed to severe stresses without suffering ill effects? Even with the stresses we have been talking about in court today?

Q: Are emotional numbing and emotional alienation always the same thing? How are they different?

Good answers to these questions call for an in-depth conceptualization of the PTSD phenomenon as a reliable and clinically significant syndrome. Responding to this last question, for example, should call for a definition of emotional numbing (assuming the term has been used or accepted by the witness), followed by an explanation of the broad range of behaviors encompassed in the term *emotional alienation*. In a similar manner, the prepared expert should routinely be able to place evaluation data in a historical and scientific context.

The same principles apply to dangerousness. For many clinicians who testify about involuntary commitments or sentencing, dangerousness is a key legal–psychological variable. Many commitment statutes demand clear, cogent, and compelling evidence of imminent violence. In some instances, case law or statutory law for involuntary commitment requires recent, demonstrable behaviors of violence or imminent violence.

Sarbin (1967) has identified dangerousness not as a behavior, but as a state of tension between people who hold power in some way and those who represent a threat to the status quo. He has asserted that dangerousness is a felt threat to one's person or property, and as a felt threat, it is the subjective experience of those who feel they have more to lose, such as valued property or other possible losses, including body integrity. My reading of the violence prediction and risk management literature is that the concept of dangerousness is too flawed for professional use in legal contexts. It is acceptable to speak of the likelihood of a suicide attempt or of the situations in which an attack on another person is most likely to occur. It is equally acceptable to speak of effects of the presence of a weapon, influences of alcohol or drug use, and the short-run likelihood of harming self or others. The word "dangerousness" carries such surplus meanings that these actual predictions of violence or harm seem preferable.

In ways like PTSD, dangerousness is a social construct that reaches far beyond the behaviors that are of legal–psychological concern. This perspective may be applied to many other psychological constructs, as well. For experts testifying on these topics, PTSD and dangerousness are best thought of more broadly than the immediate person assessed, and experts need to appreciate the development and limitations of the constructs.

The Maxim: Psychological disorders and labels are socially constructed, and the prepared expert knows the nature and limits of the constructs.

36

Taints

IN MOST COURTS, EXPERT WITNESSES can reasonably expect to be treated with respect and with minimal inquiry into their personal lives. Now and then, an attorney who is naturally intrusive, who is desperate, or who has an important case will pry into personal elements in the backgrounds of the witnesses. At their worst, these instances touch on acutely sensitive topics.

As we approach this topic, we should keep in mind that most of us have events in our lives we do not wish to have raised in open court. Lying and cheating in high school and college are more common than not in the lives of most people. Accusations (unjustified as well as justified) of wrongdoing and inappropriate behaviors mark the lives of a substantial number of people. Hard-working, highly-motivated attorneys or their staff investigators can bring personal unpleasantness to light in court. The specific outcome of such inquiries during depositions or cross-examinations is the uncomfortable appearance of being tainted that can compete with witness credibility.

Consider, for example, the woman psychologist who was testifying in a child abuse trial in one northwestern state. She had been divorced some years earlier. The opposing attorney sent an investigator to search out the divorce papers and issues that were on record. The investigator found that she had alleged that her husband at the time had been abusing their children. The investigator then obtained from the ex-husband an affidavit stating that his ex-wife, this expert witness, saw cases of child abuse behind every tree. The affidavit was admitted in court with the result that the affidavit and associated questions thoroughly embarrassed and discomforted the woman during the cross-examination.

The hurt from this cross-examination so stayed with this woman that when she spoke to me about it years after it happened, she was still emotionally anguished. Why? Because she felt awful about such a personal matter being raised in court. Because she felt the accusation in open court by her ex-husband brought all the unresolved anger from their divorce into open court. Because she felt there was no good way to dissipate the ex-husband's accusations. Her denial seemed defensive to her and her explanations felt as if they came across as strained and perhaps implausible.

At one of my workshops on court testimony a shy, soft-spoken man asked if he could speak to me privately. He had been accused of child abuse 7 months earlier, an allegation he vigorously denied. An investigation by the police and by Child Protective Services led both agencies to conclude it was a groundless accusation, and, indeed, the man had been retained by Child Protective Services to continue to do psychological evaluations and to testify in court for them. He was certain, given the newspaper publicity about the accusation, that one of the first questions to be asked by opposing counsel would be "Are you the Dr. Jones who has been accused of child abuse by the county District Attorney's Office?"

How should a wrongly accused individual reply to such a question? The dilemma would be similar whether he was rightly or wrongly accused.

In this instance, a simple and nondefensive "yes" by Dr. Jones would certainly be accurate. The witness could hope that the issue would be defused during redirect or, even better, to have been anticipated and addressed during the beginning of the direct examination. However, that initial admission might leave the court with an impression that could negatively taint the rest of the testimony, no matter how otherwise useful it was. A better reply might take the form of an admit–deny, in which the true part of the question is affirmed, and the untrue implication is strongly denied.

Thus, to the question, "Are you the Dr. Jones who has been accused of child abuse by the county District Attorney's Office?" the answer might be "Although I was indeed accused, the accusation was promptly dropped with apologies, and I have a letter on file from the police investigator apologizing for any harm that might have been done to me by this hurtful and unwarranted accusation."

Common taints on witnesses' reputations are from complaints filed to state licensing boards or ethics committees, or from lawsuits filed against witnesses. People who have never found themselves in these situations should understand that no real violation needs to have occurred for a complaint to be filed. Psychologists who do child custody work are familiar with the intense nature of feelings that lead to frequent complaints. The large majority of complaints filed with state licensing boards lead to dismissal of the complaint or minimal penalties. Practitioners who use collection agencies for long-overdue bills should equally be aware that the major single cause of lawsuits and ethics board complaints filed against clinicians is about billing, often for invasion of privacy by turning unpaid bills over to a third party for collection (despite clients signing initial consent forms allowing this possibility).

Let us assume that opposing counsel is aware of some negative allegation about an expert. A few attorneys will routinely check the files of the county or superior court in the experts' home communities to see whether any judgments against them have been filed. If asked "Isn't it true that a lawsuit alleging unprofessional practices has been filed against you in county court?" the following are two possible answers:

"Actually, a far-fetched and unfounded suit has been filed by an ex-client who would not pay the therapy fees on which we had agreed," or the more emotional "I take great pride in my professional work and my commitment to ethical practice, and such false claims are simply offensive and wrong."

These possible responses do not alleviate the pain involved in allegations of personal and professional misconduct. Three friends of mine at different times have been accused of trying to swindle an insurance company, of being unfairly biased in a custody assessment, and of conducting an incomplete evaluation as demonstrated by a brief report. As these individuals went through the various hearings and panels, meetings with lawyers, and going over and over the facts of their cases, their lives became disrupted. They became angry, depressed, or anxious, or all three; they were shunned by some colleagues; their referrals dropped off; and their personal lives were devastated by these allegations. All of them were experienced witnesses. Yet when these charges were raised during occasions of their testimony in court, and even when the court ruled the issue was not relevant, they were distressed by the experience.

There is no simple answer. Each of these psychologists has spent a long time working through the distress, and residual effects still remain. Nevertheless, we should note that such allegations can be made about anyone, and that part of our work lends itself to having disappointed clients or participants in legal processes who are unhappy with our opinions and who seek revenge. Perhaps replies to questions about tainted pasts should include explaining to the court that it is now a common part of clinical and medical practice to be the target of unfounded charges by unhappy clients.

The Maxim: Questions about allegations of misconduct should be met forthrightly, indignantly, and openly.

37

Tape Recording of Evaluations

TWO COLLEAGUES AND I WROTE an article about testifying in child abuse allegation cases stating firmly that all psychological assessments of the children involved should be recorded on videotape (Brodsky, Kruh, & Hovey, 1996). The rationale seemed simple (and, of course, it was hardly original to us). In many cases children's self-reports are the only data on which a criminal case proceeds, and, especially with young children, results of professional interviews with the children become essential pieces of evidence. For those reasons, we argued, all conscientious interviewers should videotape their interviews, and those videotapes should routinely be made available to the court to see if leading questions or other self-fulfilling inquiries were made. If interviewers can be challenged on the basis of flawed interview techniques, we argued that is how it should be. We all should be held accountable for our methods of obtaining data and how we draw conclusions.

In my own forensic evaluations, I do not routinely use tape recordings (although I should add that I do not do investigatory interviews about abuse with children). Thus, it was a very different experience to be on the other side when my uncle, Dr. Carroll Brodsky, a psychiatrist who also holds a PhD in Anthropology, made the case for audio tape recording all forensic interviews.

Carroll is someone to whom I look for professional feedback and personal advice. Thus, when Carroll argued for taping of all evaluation interviews, my interest was piqued, and I began to think about this issue in the additional context of protecting the examiner. Carroll wrote that the validity of expert opinions depends, at least in part, on having a complete and accurate record of the data from which the opinion was formed. He argued against the most common method, the one I use, which is to write down in a permanent record as much as I can of what the evaluee says as quickly and accurately as possible. A second approach, which some others use, is to dictate the details of the evaluee's statements immediately afterwards. However, the third possibility is to tape record the entire examination. Carroll wrote (personal communication, June 7, 1998):

> I would recommend the latter approach, tape recording, for several reasons. First, it is inarguably the most complete and accurate. Secondly, it resolves confusion or disputes about what either the subject or the examiner said in the course of the examination. Subjects, after reading a psychiatrist's report, frequently complain that they were misquoted or that statements they made were omitted, or that the psychiatrist asked questions that were not reflected in the report. A tape recording and a transcript based on it protect the psychiatrist against allegations of dishonesty and unprofessional behavior.
>
> Some examples make the point. A male subject whom I had examined for the defense in the course of his Workers' Compensation claim reported to a psychiatrist who examined him at the request of his own attorney that I had asked him if he had ever "slept" with his mother. He complained that this upset him so much that his mental state had deteriorated even further. In his own report, the claimant's psychiatrist characterized my conduct in asking this question of a disturbed man as unprofessional, and damaging to the subject, and indicated that the subject would need long-term treatment to deal with this trauma.
>
> A transcript of the tape recording made during the examination revealed the following as the exchange that occurred:
>
> Me: Are you married?

Subject: Don't you want to know if I ever slept with my mother?

Me: No. I don't want to know if you slept with your mother. I just want to know if you are married.

Subject: Well, I never slept with my mother.

After submitting the transcript and offering the tape, I heard nothing more about my outrageous and unprofessional behavior.

Another example was the case of a woman who claimed her employment had been terminated because of my report and that I had not warned her that what she told me during the interview would not be considered confidential. The tape recording revealed that I had not only warned her this at the beginning of the tape, but that I then asked this well educated, English-speaking woman if she understood that it was not confidential.

Subjects and patients forget some of what they said and what they heard. Psychiatrists forget some of what they say and what they hear. Tape recordings protect both subject and examiner, and I recommend that examiners use them whenever possible, and that they urge the examinees to make their own tape recordings.

This last suggestion for clients to make their own tape recordings has a special appeal. It fits closely with the polemic that Constance Fischer and I wrote (Fischer & Brodsky, 1978) in which we urged professionals to share the real power and substantial content they accumulate with the individuals with whom they work. Allowing clients to tape-record evaluation sessions does carry the risk that we may be held accountable for everything we say and ask in an evaluation, but such accountability can improve what we do.

The first suggestion, that as evaluators we should tape our sessions, prompted me to plan on taping my next assessment, which was with an imprisoned man. I asked the attorney who had retained me to do this assessment if she had any objection. "I certainly do!" she replied immediately. "I do not want anything my client says to you to be potentially discoverable, especially if I decide not to call you to testify. Do not tape-record! Period." I didn't debate the issue of discovery rules, although I was tempted, nor did I tape-record the assessment.

Despite this decision on my part, I find the case for taping to be a sensible, but not mandatory, procedure. A permanent record is developed of the interview. There will be instances in which opposing counsel learns of the tapes and seeks to obtain them during discovery. In the cases of subpoenas *duces tecum*, which call for all documents and records to be produced, compelling legal reasons exist to produce the tapes even if the tape itself has not been reviewed and even if the tape itself has not been used as part of one's findings or conclusions. Nevertheless, some evaluators may well wish to follow my uncle's suggestions, and for purposes of developing a permanent record and for self-protection, to experiment with tape-recorded sessions.

The Maxim: Evaluations that are tape-recorded may be useful for maintaining an accurate and accountable record of questions and statements of both examiners and subjects.

38

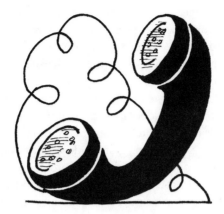

Telephone and Videotape Testimony[13]

T HIS WAS MY PSYCHOLOGIST friend's second day of testimony. The
first day had been live testimony; and a second day of testimony was given by telephone. On the first day, he had driven for
4 hours to the trial, was called by the defense, had testified in court
for over 4 hours, and then had driven home. Because of his other
commitments, all parties had reached a consensus that his testimony could continue by telephone on the second day.

This litigation revolved around whether a child had been
sexually abused. The testimony this expert witness had presented
was that the frequent masturbation by the child was not a definitive
sign of sexual abuse. The judge in this bench trial believed that
such sex play in very young children was abnormal. During his
telephone testimony on the second day, the witness cited base rate
data indicating that such sex play actually was slightly (but not
significantly) more common in nonabused than abused children.
The judge did rule for the defense, but never accepted the expert's
conclusions offered on the second day.

Afterwards, the expert felt it had been futile to try to testify

---

[13]Thanks are due to the expert, Stu Greenberg, for sharing this case.

in an effective way about a crucially important issue without being able to see the judge or the attorneys or to use demonstrative evidence. Even though the court ruled there had not been convincing evidence of abuse, the expert was aware that presenting persuasively informative testimony was notably harder for him without nonverbal feedback.

Trial testimony by telephone is less common than the other forms of telephone and videotaped testimony. The more common kinds are depositions by telephone, administrative hearings in which one testifies by telephone, and videotaped testimony in trials and depositions. It is not unusual for the professionals with whom I speak to have had unsatisfactory experiences in these physically removed events—that is, removed from being present in person at the moment of trial.

What happens? How do things go wrong? And what does it take to make them go right? A participant in one of my expert witness tutorials spoke of his role in a hearing to allow an arguably emotionally unstable worker to be reinstated to work in a nuclear power plant. His testimony was by telephone. This expert witness had been remarkably competent in a variety of other hearings, but in this testimony he had moments of feeling profoundly helpless and incompetent. When asked about the causes, he reported a sense of not being in control of his testimony. Questions came suddenly. Interruptions had no obvious location. He felt swept away by events outside his visual control.

Another witness who testified by phone in a child custody dispute reported similar difficulties. She had felt far less competent in her presentation of professional knowledge by telephone.

Not all of the variance for such helplessness lies within the witness. We should not underestimate the overall psychological climate of a trial or hearing, and how physical presence contributes to the sense of mastery. Both of these individuals customarily operated from a close synthesis of visual and auditory cues, and they were cut off from accustomed information. Testimony by telephone works best for witnesses who are predominantly aural, and works least well for individuals who are heavily dependent on what they see to form a meaningful gestalt. Speaking by telephone does not lend the power of physical presence for persuasion, for the elements that generalize to likability and credibility, and for the compelling impressiveness that attractiveness, size, clothing, stature, facial expression, and gesture can contribute.

Greater chances for misunderstandings and deficient communication occur when one testifies by telephone. Argyle, Lalljee, and Cook (1968) conducted research studies on nonverbal communication in which views of participants were fully or partially blocked. They found that bad communication, as indicated by interruptions, was most common when eye contact was blocked. Think for yourself how comfortable you are dealing with personal issues on the telephone; if you are one of those people who becomes distant and removed by phone, then you should plan on working on the medium as well as the message before any such testimony is given.

Such distance is not bad necessarily for everyone who testifies. For some witnesses, the use of physical absence can promote effectiveness. What has happened on Internet discussion groups dramatically demonstrates this outcome. Otherwise shy and diffident people sometimes blossom into flamboyant and engaging characters in the mixed personal–impersonal structure of having keyboards, screens, and anonymity between themselves and their distant companions.

For whom can telephone and videotaped testimony make a positive difference? Improvement in testifying can be observed in witnesses who are overly anxious (as opposed to just-right anxious) on the stand. With the physical presence of others and the heightened consciousness of being watched, much tension is mobilized. The less threatening forms of testifying by telephone and on tape works for some anxious and uncertain witnesses, because visual anonymity can protect them. It is not that anxiety is not generated, but the reduction of it is palpable.

When I testify by phone, I lean back in my recliner chair, close my eyes, focus fully on the content, and relax. During phone depositions I have found myself making statements such as "let us get back on task" that I would never otherwise offer.

For me, it feels good to communicate my testimony by telephone. I know witnesses who prefer unequivocally to use a good quality speakerphone; with their hands free, they feel freer, and perform better as a result.

Testifying by videotape has decidedly different qualities

than live testimony or telephone testimony. The small group that is present can be more relaxing for some witnesses. On the other hand, the presence of the camera, the recorder, and, especially, the TV monitor can potentially increase anxiety levels. For me it makes the experience better. I try not to ham it up for the camera (although the temptation is there). I do look directly into the camera as part of looking around at the participants, treating the unseen audience with attention equal to that of the visible audience.

For extroverts like me, this videotaped forum can provide an opportunity to display one's knowledge and findings to a mystery audience. For self-conscious individuals who are less at home testifying by telephone and on videotape, I have three specific suggestions:

Practice with an audio- and then videotape recorder in simulated testimony, with a colleague on hand who has prepared likely questions in advance.

Really learn if you are more comfortable talking on the phone than face to face, and plan from there. Know your own telephone and videotape comfort level versus your comfort level in live, on-site testimony.

With the permission of the parties involved, have a colleague or student listen on another line, and take notes. This opportunity for feedback and learning can be implemented using both telephones and videotape recorders.

It is likely that courts and attorneys will be using more telephone and videotaped depositions and testimony as they are faced with rising costs of bringing experts on-site (or going to the experts, in depositions) and the complex problems of arranging dockets. Experts should evaluate their own skills and preferences as they decide whether to attempt to avoid distance testimony if it serves them badly, or to encourage it if it serves them well. Because some experts will have no choice about giving testimony at a distance, getting comfortable and skilled at such testimony is a practical part of furthering one's effectiveness as an expert witness.

The Maxim: Rather than feeling disempowered by the absence of visual cues in telephone and videotape testimony, seek by practice and training to master your performance in the medium.

39

To Cry, to Faint

A T THE ONSET OF expert witness workshops, I ask participants to write down their worst experiences on the witness stand and what they most fear. One participant wrote that his worst experience was when he fainted on the stand, and another participant wrote that her greatest fear was that she would cry when challenged on the stand. The first participant's fainting was followed by a quick call to the paramedics and the witness being taken away on a stretcher. At the emergency room, he was examined and told there was nothing physically wrong and that it was a reaction to stress.

Fainting on the stand is a truly rare event, and I had never heard of it before. Fainting may have many causes, of course, but let us assume that one has had a thorough medical examination and has been unequivocally cleared of physical and pathological causes (not necessarily an easy assumption). What then for the fainter? The ways to address this possibility then become similar to that of the person who is afraid she may cry on the stand.

Let me discuss one related incident that I observed firsthand. A PhD student in my department was defending her dissertation proposal in the preliminary examination that serves as students' major hurdle for admission to candidacy. She stood frozen in place in front of the examining committee for 10 minutes, unable to present, speak, or move. This 10 minutes seemed like hours to the committee and, probably, like a lifetime to the student. Then a tear rolled from her right eye down her cheek. It was followed by another tear, and then a rush of other tears, only from the right eye, while the student stood otherwise emotionless and immobile in the room.

My first suggestion is for individuals who find themselves truly likely to cry or faint at stressful moments: Try not to put yourself in a situation in which you are called to testify. Crying or even simple tearfulness is enough to undermine the worth of even the most compelling scholarly evidence. At one time a student of mine would carry on rational and articulate conversations with an even, controlled tone of voice while tears ran from her eyes. Her thoughts were sound, but her audiences were skeptical and distracted, despite her occasional statements that this tearfulness was a behavior of no emotional consequence. (At a later time, after finishing her degree, she acknowledged how the tears were indeed a literal leaking through of distressed vulnerability in her otherwise intact veneer of control.)

The advice I would offer in general for other witnesses afraid of fainting and crying on the stand is to habituate to the setting. As often as not, judges allow expert witnesses to sit in the courtroom for testimony other than their own. Watching this trial unfold, and other trials as well, allows the witness to see the ordinariness of the courtroom events that transpire, how variable and often ineffective attorneys are, and how to grasp the otherwise personally unfamiliar events and roles in trials.

Habituation to the demands on an expert is a good idea for first time witnesses in general. For people who are fearful of crying or fainting, or with an occasional history of these occurrences in other stressful situations, it becomes essential.

To ameliorate the problem, find an ally. To be desensitized to the courtroom, it helps to be accompanied by a knowledgeable and experienced compatriot. Choose an ally with a matter-of-fact understanding of trials who can explain and comment with a comfortable and active sharing. If you happen on a legal or psychological ally who can discuss courtroom carryings-on with serenity and reassurance, all the better. However, almost any experienced and perceptive person can accompany and reassure you. Furthermore, be aware of how often court testimony is not challenged or difficult. It is like a monster-under-the-bed fear or anxiety about a first verbal book report in elementary school. The anxiety about the monster or report is far greater than the real threat from the monster or class.

By themselves, the habituation, the understanding, the ally, and the broader perspective may diminish the threats and uncertainty of testifying. The question still remains of what to do if you are on the stand and suddenly find that you are feeling faint or are about to cry. Under those circumstances, take care of yourself. For most of us, there are a few standard techniques we have mastered to help us with stressful moments. For me, the techniques include deep, relatively controlled breathing, which tends to produce relaxed, relatively controlled responses. Before you go to testify, review in your mind what your best characteristic methods are for mastering anxiety, and commit yourself to using them. Of course, being thoroughly prepared for the case will go a long way toward reducing levels of anxiety.

A more active and interventionist behavior is to call things to a temporary halt in a way that fits with court customs. You do not have to simply sit, reply to questions, and feel increasingly out of control. It is altogether okay to turn to the judge and say "Your honor, would it be possible for us to take a very brief break right now for personal reasons? I would appreciate it." The judge will not ask what the personal reasons are; after all, you have already described them as personal in nature, and the judge does not want to know if you have an urgent need to get to a rest room, or whether you have just remembered that you need to check up on child-care arrangements. You have stated that you need to stop, that the stopping needs to be now, and that it is personal. Most judges will readily accede to your request. This break time will permit a chance to compose yourself and be able to resume more comfortably.

The Maxim: Address fears of crying and fainting on the stand by habituating to the courtroom, by drawing on an ally, by gaining perspective, and by calling for a break in your testimony, if necessary.

40

Traps of Common Sense

I N ONE MEMORABLE CASE I had been retained and called to testify by the plaintiff's attorney in a malpractice and wrongful death trial. After the direct examination was completed, the defense attorney began to cross-examine me step by step, with each question carefully designed to permit me only a yes or no answer. Her questions were framed in terms that led listeners to think they would know what the answers would be, because "simple common sense" would point in that direction.

The first question asked if the defendant, Dr. Z., had seen the deceased patient on over 100 occasions.

I agreed.

"Wasn't it true that Dr. Z. had much more exposure to the patient than you had?"

"Yes."

"Isn't it true that your knowledge was only based on documentation?"

"Yes, most certainly, because the patient is dead."

At this point, with satisfaction in her tone of voice at having me cornered, the attorney asked this next question, with a measured assuredness of what my answer would be:

"Isn't the clinical interview with its direct, personal contact the best source of knowledge about a patient?"

"No," I replied firmly.

The cross-examining attorney was nonplused. She asked the question again in another way. I said "no" once again. In a frustrated outburst, she asked what I could possibly know from documentation that would be as good or better than a personal, clinical interview.

"The patient's history," I answered, "third party information, results of tests administered by several different psychologists, behavior observations in the record. The whole unfolding of this patient's life, as his pathology developed, became visible, made its way into actions, shaped his emotional and cognitive life, and then led to his suicide."

The attorney had been certain she was in control because she was relying on the trap of common sense. This trap depends on the witness acquiescing to a statement because it seems obviously true, until one really thinks about it along directly related scientific or professional dimensions.

Perlin (1994) has addressed this susceptibility to common-sense thinking that is actually false in nature. In a scathing attack on the use of Ordinary Common Sense (OCS) in criminal courts and especially in insanity pleas, Perlin noted that OCS is not only an incomplete and imperfect tool, but also is supported neither by empirical investigations nor underlying theory. Perlin concluded

> Excessive reliance on OCS infects all players in the drama. Careful research studies have thus found that judges, attorneys, legislators, and mental health professionals all inappropriately employ irrelevant stereotypical negative information in coming to conclusions on the related question of the potential future dangerousness of a mentally disabled criminal defendant. What we *call* "common sense" is frequently nothing more than sanism: the irrational thought processes, founded on stereotype, that are at the roots of our incoherent insanity defense jurisprudence. (pp. 295–296)

Our present operational definition of common sense will consist of unsupported conclusions that seem true to most observers. In all courtroom testimony, this lure of common sense may be thought of as a commonsense heuristic, that is, a speculative but deeply held rule-of-thumb that serves to guide and organize thinking.

Psychology abounds with commonsense heuristics. The seminal articles dissecting these heuristics were the ones by Chapman and Chapman (1969), who identified commonsense errors in test interpretation. The Chapmans applied the notion of illusory correlations to the interpretation of selected projective tests, in which the commonsense heuristic was the operating principle. Other researchers have since taken illusory correlation research much further (Berndsen, van der Pligt, Spears, & McGarty, 1996; deJong, Merckelbach, Boegels, & Kindt, 1998).

Take, for example, human-figure drawings in which adult clients place sharp teeth on the figures they draw. Common sense "informs" us that sharp teeth are associated with hostility or anger, and, indeed, with that assumption in hand, test interpreters infer that the clients themselves are hostile or angry. These conclusions have often been made for adult clients whose hostility is otherwise unremarkable. For some evaluators, this sharp-teeth-equals-hostility link has been maintained even in the light of research findings that fail to link drawings with adult personality and psychopathology. Indeed, Hammer and Piotrowski (1953) have observed a decided relationship between hostility of the test interpreters and amount of hostility they see in human-figure drawings. Thus, we should remember that unexamined "professional sense" may not be supported by scholarly literature.

As mental health professionals and academics, we tend to be more skilled at identifying such heuristics in the literature and in other clinicians than in questions by attorneys during cross-examinations. What happens on the stand is that psychologists often fall prey to the commonsense demand rather than the scholarly context of the question.

Two additional commonsense cross-examination questions may serve to illustrate this process:

"With all that was at stake, wasn't the defendant (or plaintiff) motivated to give an impression of abnormality?"

The beginning part of this question is the commonsense link. However, experts need to recall and report how impression management by the defendant or plaintiff is not necessarily a motivated, slanted presentation of self, but often an intrinsic part of oneself.

"Your opinion is only just that, an opinion, isn't it?"

This commonsense query is intended to reduce the power of expert testimony. One way of replying is to state "No, it is my best professional judgment."

Good responses to commonsense heuristics seek to displace the seeming rule of thumb with professional knowledge. Ineffective responses unthinkingly embrace the commonsense assumptions and lead witnesses into self-contradictory statements.

The Maxim: Do not be immediately agreeable to affirmations of common sense until you have thought through the specific meanings of the questions for your data, conclusions, and opinions.

41

Trivial Pursuits

IN SOME CROSS-EXAMINATIONS and especially in depositions, questions are asked that stump the expert witnesses. The questions may be about some minor aspect of professional practice. They may be about continuing controversies such as prescription privileges or managed care in cases that have nothing to do with either issue. The questions may also be about items in the licensing examination, about international differences in training, or about whether the current president of APA was correct in his or her assertions.

Like most professionals who end up in court or depositions, I have sat through such irrelevant questioning. The one common element in all such inquiries is that there is no obvious connection to the issues about which I was called to testify. Still, there are different ways to think about these questions and to prepare oneself to respond to them. Let us consider them in order from the most catastrophizing to the least catastrophizing interpretations of what may be occurring in the courtroom.

SUSPICIONS OF AN INGENIOUS SET-UP

This reaction assumes that the attorneys are goal-directed in their apparently trivial questions, moving with clever indirection toward some major confrontation or revelation. Questions about eyewitness accuracy or the Stanford Prison Experiment would thus become revealed as a successful circumnavigation of the witnesses' guard, so that the answers will result in an unknowing admission that contradicts a scientific or professional opinion already in evidence or known. Sometimes witnesses fear that their answers will serve as a reflection of how little they know. Witnesses who make these assumptions become mountain-militia suspicious of each question, and this suspiciousness by itself tends to make witnesses unnaturally evasive and ineffective.

CONTINUING LEGAL EDUCATION (CLE) RIPPLES

Imagine the opposing attorneys in a sexual harassment civil action asking these questions that appear substantive but that are unrelated to anything in the case:

"Is meta-analysis an important part of psychological science?"

"What is an effect size?"

"Do findings become more accepted by the scientific community when they are supported by meta-analysis?"

"What are the major alternatives to meta-analysis in integrating the results of many scientific studies?"

"How many studies do you consider necessary in a meta-analysis before you will accept the meta-analysis as an accurate finding?"

One tenable interpretation of these questions is that opposing counsel has either attended a continuing legal education (CLE) course or has otherwise been exposed to the scientific case for meta-analysis of complex studies. If witnesses are not knowledgeable about meta-analysis, I hope they would reply with as many "I don't know" answers as their lack of knowledge merits.

Sometimes the examples and questions reflect a narrow interest that the attorneys have brought to the courtroom from their CLE courses. For example, it is possible in a custody hearing that the questions could focus on the parents' attention to, and control over, aspartame or coenzyme Q-10 or organically grown produce in the children's diet, as if these molecular issues are the essence of good parenting. In one child custody hearing Mark Mays (personal communication, January 8, 1999) reported listening to an extended and contentious debate over whether serving "Lucky Charms" breakfast cereal was indicative of neglect by one of the parents.

The aware expert listens with care and responds only to the limits of her or his knowledge, as well as placing the answers in context when the opportunity arises. An example of context is "I know of no psychological or nutritional literature that suggests that ensuring coenzyme Q-10 in a child's diet marks careful and responsible parenting."

ATTORNEYS' PERSONAL FOCUSES

Sometimes attorneys ask about a trivial topic because it is their personal focus and preoccupation. For reasons highly idiosyncratic and nonobvious, or as a result of a singular success in a prior case, a concept or practice has galvanized their attention. For them, everything connects to Co-E Q-10 and nutrition, or to the writings of John Monahan, or John Grisham, or John Dunne. This practice is especially noticeable in depositions where attorneys may follow these preoccupations for as long as they wish.

These inquiries are relatively easy to parry, so long as they are understood for what they are: solely about the attorneys' interests or preoccupations. Unlike the content that may emerge from Continuing Legal Education courses, this content is more obviously off-task, and more readily answered with statements that the content was not addressed in the assessment and is not addressed in one's professional work.

THE UNFOCUSED PURSUIT

Novice expert witnesses, in particular, tend to give much undeserved credit to examining attorneys for planning their questions. Although some attorneys are clearly and effectively on task, many use depositions as part of a general poking and prying exercise. Their questions are not intended to produce a specific outcome, but rather are intended to see what areas become productive and worth pursuing. During depositions attorneys will sometimes delve into details of undergraduate courses taken by the witnesses years ago, or into particular presentations made about unrelated topics that appeared on the witnesses' CV ("Doctor, tell us what was in the talk you gave about the history and development of primate laboratories in Florida"). After all, opposing counsel is paying for experts' time during depositions, and counsel may indeed ask where the witnesses have traveled, what their earlier careers have been, and what television shows they watch.

What to do in these circumstances?

My advice is to take it as it comes. As tempting as it may be to correct the attorney by stating firmly "that question is irrelevant," relevance is the court's business and not ours. Asserting what is relevant, thus, is outside the scope of our expertise, and could be interpreted as arrogant. Instead, try answering as clearly as possible within the limits of professional or scientific knowledge. Do not answer on the basis of an article in the *Wall Street Journal*, or even *The New York Times*. Answer only if the knowledge is part of your scholarly and professional expertise. For example, I am a vegetarian and read about health and diet issues in my personal search to find a balanced intake of proteins, vitamins, and minerals. However, I would never think of presenting this personal knowledge as part of my expertise as a psychologist.

When deposition questions become truly trivial, such as what television shows I watch, I stay aware that one option is to turn to retaining counsel and ask about answering the question. At that point, the attorneys would parry back and forth, and the typical outcome is advice from retaining counsel to answer only if I wish to. For that reason, it is useful to think on my own when the question is asked if I wish to answer it.

Do I wish to answer? With the awareness that few of these questions are task-oriented, I answer many such questions. I am not a secretive person by nature, and talking about my television habits, travel experiences, and what little I remember from undergraduate courses are all well within my tolerance for comfortable disclosure. Witnesses more private about their lives may wish to respond, "I have not based my assessment, findings, or opinion in any way on my television watching habits." Sometimes that statement closes the topic.

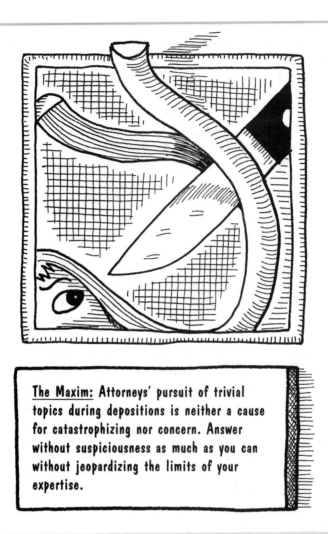

The Maxim: Attorneys' pursuit of trivial topics during depositions is neither a cause for catastrophizing nor concern. Answer without suspiciousness as much as you can without jeopardizing the limits of your expertise.

42

Ultimate Opinion Testimony

WHEN I PUT OUT A CALL on the psychology and law Internet discussion list[14] for testifying experiences that would be instructive, I fully expected that most of the replies would be about aggressive cross-examinations. Instead, the majority of responses were about ultimate issue testimony. The specialty guidelines and articles in the literature have indicated that experts should not testify on ultimate legal issues, because these issues belong to the triers of fact and are typically seen as beyond the proper reach of expert testimony. Yet, the case for or against it is far from settled, and some evidence rules about this vary by jurisdiction. Let us begin with two instances in which the court has instructed witnesses to give opinions as to ultimate issues.

Psychologist Howie Lester wrote of his first experience testifying on a court-ordered competency to stand trial evaluation.

> Being very caught up at that time in the "ivory tower"
> vs "working in the trenches" ethical discussions, I offered clinical data relevant to the issue, but no ultimate

---

[14]Subscriptions to this PSYLAW-L list may be obtained by contacting Steve Penrod at spenrod1@unl.edu.

opinion. The judge pressed me on the issue. I told him
I would offer an opinion if he insisted, but I preferred
to leave that matter to the court. He told me he would
not order me to offer an opinion, but then added: "Since
you're taking an ethical stance, you can stand on your
ethics in that corner of my courtroom until you decide
to volunteer an opinion." I immediately gave him an
opinion. It was my birthday. I wanted to go home. I
didn't see this as humorous at the time. I was sure I'd
done wrong. After many years "in the trenches," well,
let's just say I've mellowed.

Note two aspects of this description. First, Dr. Lester indicated that he would give the ultimate opinion if the judge insisted;
that comment may have been heard as an invitation for the judge
to insist. Second, Dr. Lester indicated that he had "mellowed," presumably in his harsh judgment of himself, or he now viewed that
instance and others of ultimate issue opinions as acceptable.

In another example, Dr. Joe Dixon also was asked to testify
as to ultimate opinion, this time in a mental responsibility defense.
Dr. Dixon described it this way:

Several years ago, when I was a new forensic "expert,"
I had evaluated the defendant in a felony case[15] and was
on the stand nearing the end of my cross examination
by the defense attorney in this bench trial. The courtroom was crowded, the judge was attentive, and, thus
far, the questioning by both attorneys had been on point
and knowledgeable. The defense attorney then asked
me for an ultimate issue opinion.

"So, Doctor, you are telling this court that Mr. Smith
was insane at the time of this offense?"

---

[15] The defendant had come up behind a woman who was waiting for a cab on a
busy downtown street corner. He had lifted her dress over her head, she screamed,
lost her balance, and fell, injuring her ankle. The defendant remained where he was
until a nearby doorman tackled him and pinned him down until the police arrived.
The defendant was a 40-year-old unemployed man with a chronic history of schizophrenia and homelessness. He had no explanation as to why he had done such a
thing, but readily admitted he must have done it, because the police wouldn't lie.
The District Attorney had painted a picture of a lurking menace who was preying
on innocent women.

I quickly deferred, and began to explain such a conclusion was the prerogative and province exclusively of the court. The judge interrupted me, and said, "No, that's quite all right, Doctor, please answer the question."

At that point the District Attorney leaped to his feet and objected. What ensued was a heated three way debate for several minutes in open court over whether an expert could or could not offer an opinion on insanity. Finally, the gavel came down hard with the judge glaring at both attorneys.

"Sit down," he instructed. He then turned to me, and in a kindly voice said, "Go ahead, doctor, now answer the question. Was he or was he not insane at the time?" I reiterated that my ethics and training simply would not allow me to offer an ultimate opinion. The judge listened quietly until I finished. I thought I had persuaded him of my point.

The judge, well over six feet tall, about 300 pounds, with penetrating, intelligent eyes, was impressively in command with his flowing black robe, gold chains, and white silk shirt. He smiled, and said, "We all hear what the good doctor is saying," and then leaning toward me, in a soft voice he continued, "but, Doctor, if you could have such an opinion, just supposing you could, hypothetically speaking, what would that opinion be, exactly?" I was so nervous, I didn't know if I was coming or going. I tried to think. Should I answer a hypothetical like this? My mind was blank, but my mouth seemed to be in its usual working order. I said, "Well, if I could, knowing what I do about the case and the circumstances, I imagine I would decide that there were grounds for a mental state defense inasmuch as he has a long history of schizophrenia, and his behavior at the time was quite disorganized. That is, the defendant was, in my opinion, insane at the time."

The defense attorney was smiling broadly, the district attorney was on his feet objecting, and the judge's gavel came down hard again, and he said, "SIT DOWN Mr. District Attorney!"

He continued: "This court thanks the good Doctor, and it is the opinion of this court that there are grounds for an insanity defense, and it is the further finding and

decision of this court that the defendant was insane at
the time of this unfortunate incident. I find the defendant, Mr. Smith, not guilty by reason of insanity and order him released to the custody of his mother. This court
is adjourned."

That was it. There were no closing arguments, and
nothing else. The judge thanked me again and excused
me. It was over; I looked up and both attorneys were
already leaving the courtroom, so I gathered my papers
and left, still in a daze as to what had happened.

Dr. Dixon concluded:

This was one of my first trials in which I testified, and I
learned what the phrase "swift justice" means. I learned
that there is the law, and then there is how judges in-
terpret the law, and there is justice after all.

It is arguable whether justice had occurred in this case. What
is clear is the similarity between the offering of an ultimate legal
conclusion and similar post-hoc analyses by both experts. But is it
proper and ethical? *The Specialty Guidelines for Forensic Psychology* (Committee on Ethical Guidelines for Forensic Psychologists,
1991) are clear on this point: such expert opinions are not proper.
The *Guidelines* indicate that in offering expert evidence, forensic
psychologists ". . . are aware that their own professional observations, inference, and conclusions must be distinguished from legal
facts, opinions, and conclusions." Despite the opening notation that
the guidelines are aspirational, in practice psychologists take the
guidelines seriously and tend to follow them to the letter. Yet, some
authorities have disagreed with the guidelines and have made statements in favor of selected and careful offering of ultimate conclusions.

For example, Fulero & Finkel (1991) reported that ultimate
issue testimony by experts does not affect jury verdicts in *not guilty
by reason of insanity* defenses. Fulero (personal communication,
1998) further asserted that it is not unethical to offer ultimate issue
testimony. He stated,

I don't fault anyone who offers their expert opinion to
a court that is requesting it. In fact, I believe that is our

job as long as we 'recognize limits to the certainty with which diagnoses, judgments, or predictions can be made about individuals.'

He urges changing the Specialty Guidelines to be consistent with what is requested and can reasonably be expected of us:

Practitioners need to change their behaviors, because to risk upsetting the courts and ultimately being excluded from the legal proceedings, is of no help whatsoever to the judicial system. (S. Fulero, Personal Communication, May 13, 1998)

He also offers this example of appropriate testimony regarding an insanity plea: "In my professional opinion, the defendant suffers from a serious mental illness as defined by the *DSM-IV*; also, as a result of my evaluation, it is my opinion that this mental disorder rendered the defendant unable to understand the wrongfulness of his actions." This testimony is still one step away from the ultimate legal conclusion that the defendant is legally insane. Fulero concluded that if we are not willing to answer these questions, as a profession we should refuse to get involved in insanity evaluations altogether, by noting that we cannot ethically respond to the referral questions (S. Fulero, personal communication, May 13, 1998).

Ray Hays (personal communication, 1998) has pointed out that in Justice Kennedy's separate concurring opinion in *United States v. Scheffer* (No. 96–1133, decided March 31, 1998) and in Rule 704(a) of the Federal Rules of Evidence, an expert opinion is allowed to embrace an ultimate issue to be decided by the trier of fact.

With all of this said, I plan to continue to avoid giving ultimate legal conclusions and to stay with the psychological conclusions. Of course, psychological assessments often are geared to approximate legal conclusions. In some instances, away from public scrutiny, psychological testimony about involuntary commitment, testamentary capacity, and contractual competency is commonly offered in terms of ultimate issues. Still, practice does not make proper, and the distinction sometimes feels awkward. At times on the stand I have felt evasive—indeed, *been* evasive—in

181

reply to ultimate issue questions. Yet, I have replied and plan to continue to reply that the ultimate issue questions are legal in nature and, therefore, beyond the limits of my expertise, training, and licensure. It is a boundary that makes sense for expert testimony.

The Maxim: Ultimate issue testimony should be approached with caution and considered a rare event that is dependent on the situation.

43

What I Don't and Do Like to See
in an Expert Witness[16]

I T IS FAR EASIER to assert the negative case of what I do not like
to see in an expert than the reverse. Much like the experience I
had with an auto salesman who would not return the keys to my
car that had been checked out for a trade-in estimate, or with the
big-name physician who insisted on patronizing me after an examination, my negative impressions about witnesses are more clear
and vivid than the positive ones. The following is a summary of
what I do not like in an expert witness.

TESTIFYING BEYOND ONE'S COMPETENCE

Managed care has produced a vocal cohort of resentful clinicians; whether the resentment is justified is, of course, arguable.
As a consequence of this dissatisfaction, a noticeable number of
independent health practitioners have moved into forensic work

---

[16] A much longer and wordier version of this chapter was presented to the General
Session of the 3rd Annual Conference for Testifying and Consulting Experts, San
Francisco, September 29, 1996.

and testimony. Forensic evaluations and testimony are free from the intrusions by managed care into independent decision-making of practitioners. For a few of these professionals, the move has been quite precipitous. Some of these experts, as well as some existing forensic experts, get in over their heads. They want their practices to be successful and they want to build up their referrals. Now and then they practice beyond their actual knowledge and expertise.

The responsible choices for such new forensic practitioners are to decline many cases or to throw themselves seriously into mastering professional competence in these new subjects. I consult by telephone to new forensic psychologists who seek guided supervision about how to acquire new competencies, a consultation that is exciting for me because they are really willing to listen, work, and to receive critical feedback. Some experts do not pursue new competencies and their actions result in the problems I address in this chapter.

One frequently sees these lapses in competencies in response to direct examination. The juries are not always aware of the deficiencies, but for testimony within my own areas of competence, I am all too aware of these glaring gaps in knowledge. I find myself wishing I could advise opposing counsel on how to proceed with the questioning. Sometimes the knowledge presented during direct examination is obsolete. Sometimes the conclusions do not follow. Sometimes the person just misses the boat on how the forensic assessment should have been done, thinking only in terms of clinical assessments.

This problem can recur during cross-examination. Some witnesses compensate for their deficiencies in knowledge through guesswork, but also through strong assertions such as "That is what I found, and that is the nature of this person." Such stubbornness in the face of one's gaps in knowledge is both distressing and avoidable, and reflects badly on the witness.

DEFENSIVENESS REPLACES CLARITY AND OPENNESS

Even among well-prepared and knowledgeable experts, being under perceived attack during cross-examination creates a tendency to be defensive. Such experts refuse to give an inch, even when it is apparent that the facts call for admitting deficits in knowledge or expertise. This defensiveness is especially true about admitting points that contradict one's conclusions. When I am in the courtroom observing this type of exchange, I want to yell out loudly "For goodness sake, give in on this point! It is not such a big deal!"

Psychologists who are sharply skilled at recognizing defensiveness in their clients and in themselves during psychotherapy may misplace those skills and awareness when they are under pressure on the stand. My advice is to incorporate such self-awareness into courtroom behaviors. When you hear yourself straining to avoid having to admit a contradiction or acknowledge a point that supports opposing counsel, pay attention. Identify the process. Then let go of it.

RABBITING ON: MOUTHS THAT NEVER STOP

Maybe it is because the witness box is rather like a pulpit. Perhaps it is because of anxiety, but whatever the cause, some witnesses cannot resist elaborating on a point. They make the point, but before the next question is asked, they say it again in a slightly different way, and then repeat it several times more. My attention fades as the testimony becomes diffused by needless elaborations. This particular behavior occurs with little awareness on the part of the witness. When I replay videotapes of mock testimony in expert witness tutorials, the participants are startled by how much they repeat themselves and how markedly it diminishes the power of their testimony.

LOSING CONFIDENCE DURING CROSS-EXAMINATION

Sometimes I see a witness wilt during cross-examination. Personal traits and states both contribute to this process of diminution. The personal traits are excessive sensitivity to criticism, combined with a professional self-concept that combines pursuit of mastery with a vulnerable inadequacy. It is not always the novice witness who is this way on the stand; sometimes good clinicians and people I hold in much respect suffer from this sense of inadequacy during cross-examination.

The state of loss of confidence often appears in the form of a weak presentation of public self when attacked. The witnesses do seem to become physically as well as psychologically diminished.

What follows is a summary of things I *like* to see in an expert.

PREPARATION

It is a pleasure to see a thoroughly prepared and knowledgeable expert. The best experts have prepared for the specific issues involved in the case, and it shows. The fallback position of some witnesses is to generalize unthinkingly from existing knowledge. Using existing knowledge is expected. However, the knowledge has to fit the issue at hand.

You may know the story of the second grade child who prepared for a biology test by studying about worms. One test question was to write about elephants. "Elephants are large animals," the child wrote, "They are very large. They are much larger than worms. Speaking of worms . . . ." The task of expert witnesses is to know about the nature of elephants in their own right, without digging up the old reliable worms that burrow around in their professional gardens.

CLEAR AND ORGANIZED TESTIMONY

Clear testimony calls for clear thinking, with advanced and organized preparation. Ineffective witnesses find themselves in a tangle on the stand as they try extemporaneously to consider the fundamental tenets of their disciplines. Effective witnesses have an organized and clear conceptualization of the fundamentals and how they apply to the case being tried. My friends and students who have seen my desk may find it odd, to say the least, that I preach organization. Finding papers on my desk takes on the character of an archeological dig. Desktops notwithstanding, good witnesses mentally organize their responses before they speak, and allow their observations and conclusions to unfold in a rational and lucid manner.

SELF-KNOWLEDGE

The best expert witnesses are aware of and comfortable with themselves and the impact of their testimony. It is elementary and obvious to say "know thyself." Nevertheless, two areas of self-knowledge serve witnesses especially well. First, know how you respond under pressure. Be aware of what happens when you are not coping well. Second, have a strategy for self-correction when your testimony is going awry. It may be your favorite focusing technique, or the use of imagery, or acting in ways that are counter-intuitive—speaking nicely when you feel angered. Whatever your particular self-correction, rehearse it sufficiently so that it is an integral part of your testimony repertoire.

COMFORTABLE ADMISSION OF WEAKNESSES

Moments appear in many trials when opposing counsel senses your weaknesses and closes in for the kill. At these moments, effective witnesses comfortably admit what it is they do not know or have not done. They are truly comfortable so that the admission is made with equanimity and interpersonal ease. When witnesses respond this way, the whole adversarial process becomes transformed into an exchange that is much better for the witnesses and much less favorable to the cross-examining attorneys. Consider this example: a friend of mine used to jog past an area in which many dogs would chase him. He would stop his run, and with commanding poise, point his arm with hand and index finger straight out at the dogs. The dogs would stop, freeze in place, and then give up the chase. So it is with witness calmness and comfort in courtroom testimony.

The Maxim: Decide for yourself what it is you dislike in yourself as an expert and what you like. Then, take active steps to diminish the aspects that do not work and enhance the ones that do.

References

Argyle, M., Lalljee, M., & Cook, M. (1968). The effect of visibility on interactions in a dyad. *Human Relations, 21,* 3–17.

Baudrillard, J. (1994). *Simulacra and simulation.* Ann Arbor: University of Michigan Press.

Berndsen, M., van der Pligt, J., Spears, R., & McGarty, C. (1996). Expectation-based and data-based illusory correlation: The effects of confirming versus disconfirming evidence. *European Journal of Social Psychology, 26,* 899–913.

Bierce, A. (1958). *The Devil's dictionary.* New York: Dover. (Original work published 1911)

Brodsky, S. L. (1991). *Testifying in court: Guidelines and maxims for the expert witness.* Washington, DC: American Psychological Association.

Brodsky, S. L. (1998). Forensic Evaluation and Testimony. In Koocher, G. P., Norcross, J. C., & Hill, S. S., III. (Eds.). *Psychologist's desk reference.* New York: Oxford University Press.

Brodsky, S. L. (1988). *The psychology of adjustment and well-being.* New York: Holt, Rinehart, and Winston.

Brodsky, S. L., Kruh, I., & Hovey, M. A. (1996). Clinical testimony about child abuse: Fears and effectiveness. *Ohio Psychologist, 43*(6), 4–6.

Bursztajn, H. J., & Brodsky, A. (1998). Ethical and effective testimony after *Daubert.* In L. E. Lifson & R. I. Simon (Eds.), *The mental health practitioner and the law: A comprehensive handbook.* Cambridge, MA: Harvard University Press.

Buss, A. H. (1980). *Self-consciousness and social anxiety.* San Francisco: Freeman.

Buss, A. H. (1988). *Personality: Evolutionary heritage and distinctiveness.* Hillsdale, NJ: Erlbaum.

Chapman, L. J., & Chapman, J. P. (1969). Illusory correlations as an obstacle to the use of valid psychodiagnostic signs. *Journal of Abnormal Psychology, 74,* 271–280.

Colbach, E. M. (1981). Integrity checks on the witness stand. *Bulletin of the American Academy of Psychiatry and Law, 9,* 285–288.

Childress, J. F. (1989). The normative principles of medical ethics. In R. M. Veatch (Ed.), *Medical ethics.* Boston: Jones & Bartlett.

Committee on Ethical Guidelines for Forensic Psychologists. (1991). Specialty guidelines for forensic psychologists. *Law and Human Behavior, 15,* 655–665.

Darling, L. (1996). For better and worse. *Esquire, 125* (No. 5; May), 58–66.

deJong, P. J., Merckelbach, H., Boegels, S., & Kindt, M. (1998). Illusory correlation and social anxiety. *Behaviour Research and Therapy, 36,* 1063–1073.

Derrida, J. (1988). *The ear of the other: Otobiography, transference, translation* (C. McDonald, Ed., P. Kamute, Trans.). Lincoln: University of Nebraska Press.

Faust, D. (1994). Are there sufficient foundations for mental health experts to testify in court? No. In S. A. Kirk & S. D. Einbinder (Eds.), *Controversial issues in mental health* (pp. 196–201). Boston: Allyn & Bacon.

Faust, D., & Ziskin, J. (1988). The expert witness in psychology and psychiatry. *Science, 241,* 31–35.

Fischer, C. T. (1994). *Individualizing psychological assessment.* Hillsdale, NJ: Lawrence Erlbaum Associates.

Fischer, C. T., & Brodsky, S. L. (Eds.). (1978). *Client participation in human services: The Prometheus principle.* New Brunswick, NJ: Transaction Books.

Ford, C. V. (1996). *Lies! Lies! Lies! The psychology of deceit.* Washington, DC: American Psychiatric Association.

Fulero, S., & Finkel, N. (1991). Barring ultimate issue testimony: An "insane" rule? *Law and Human Behavior, 15,* 495–506.

Garb, H. N. (1989). Clinical judgment, clinical training, and professional experience. *Psychological Bulletin, 105,* 387–396.

Goodman-Delahunty, J. (1997). Forensic psychological expertise in the wake of *Daubert. Law and Human Behavior, 21,* 121–140.

Goodman-Delahunty, J., & Foote, W. E. (1995). Compensation for pain, suffering, and other psychological injuries: The impact of *Daubert* on employment discrimination claims. *Behavioral Sciences and the Law, 13,* 183–206.

Grodin, C. (1990). *It would be so nice if you weren't here: My journey through showbusiness.* New York: Vintage.

Hagen, M. A. (1997). *Whores of the court: The fraud of psychiatric testimony and the rape of American Justice.* New York: ReganBooks.

Hammer, E. F., & Piotrowski, Z. A. (1953). Hostility as a factor in the clinician's personality as it affects his interpretation of projective drawings (H-T-P). *Journal of Projective Techniques, 17,* 210–216.

James, W. (1890). *The principles of psychology (Vol. 1).* New York: Holt.

Jordan, J. (1987). *Working girls: Women in the New Zealand sex industry talk to Jan Jordan.* Auckland, New Zealand: Penguin.

Kelley, D. M. (1997). Reasonable doubts (M. Pressman, Director). In D. Kelley (Producer), *the practice.* New York: American Broadcasting Company.

Kemp, S., Brodsky, S. L., & Caputo, A. A. (1997). How cruel is a cat playing with a mouse? A study of people's assessment of cruelty. *New Zealand Journal of Psychology, 26,* 19–24.

Kessler, J. (1982, August). *The curious nature of teasing.* Paper presented at the 90th Annual Convention of the American Psychological Association, Washington, DC.

Kirk, S. A., & Kutchins, H. (1992). *The selling of DSM: The rhetoric of science in psychiatry.* Hawthorne, NY: Aldine de Gruyter.

Klawans, H. L. (1991). *Trials of an expert witness: Tales of clinical neurology and the law.* Boston: Little, Brown.

Kopp, S. (1977). *Back to one: A practical guide for psychotherapists.* Palo Alto, CA: Science and Behavior Books.

Kooij, J. G. (1971). *Ambiguity in natural language: An investigation of certain problems in its linguistic description.* Amsterdam: North-Holland.

Lee, H. (1960). *To kill a mockingbird.* Philadelphia: Lippincott.

Lembcke, J. L. (1997, August). From sadness to madness: Vietnam veterans and the social construction of post-traumatic stress disorder. Presented at the Annual Meeting of the American Sociological Association, Toronto.

Levy, B. (1997). *Real and apparent ambiguities.* Montreal: Barry Levy.

Lubet, S. (1998, April). Reconstructing Atticus Finch. Paper presented at the School of Law, The University of Alabama, Tuscaloosa.

Malandro, L. A., Barker, L., & Barker, D. A. (1989). *Nonverbal communication, 2nd ed.* New York: Random House.

Matson, J. V. (1990). *Effective expert witnessing: A handbook for technical professionals.* Chelsea, MI: Lewis.

Perlin, M. L. (1994). *The jurisprudence of the insanity defense.* Durham, NC: Carolina University Press.

Prochaska, J. O., & Norcross, J. C. (1994). *Systems of psychotherapy: A transtheoretical approach.* Pacific Grove, CA: Brooks/Cole.

Rappeport, J. R. (1993). Ethics and the expert witness. *Hospital and Community Psychiatry, 44,* 390–391.

Richardson, J., Dobbin, S., Gatowski, S., Ginsburg, G., & Merlino, M. (1998, March). *A case law survey of social and behavioral science evidence after Daubert.* Paper presented at the Biennial Meeting of the American Psychology-Law Society, Redondo Beach, CA.

Saarinen, A. (1981). Quantifier phrases are (at least) five ways ambiguous in intensional contexts. In F. Heny (Ed.), *Ambiguities in intensional contexts.* Dordrecht, Holland: D. Reidel.

Sales, B. D., & Shuman, D. W. (1993). Reclaiming the integrity of science in expert witnessing. *Ethics & Behavior, 3,* 223–229.

Salter, A. C. (1998). Confessions of a whistle-blower: Lessons learned. *Ethics and Behavior, 8,* 115–124.

Sarbin, T. (1967). The dangerous individual: An outcome of social identity transformations. *British Journal of Criminology, 7,* 285–295.

Schultz-Ross, R. A. (1993). Ethics and the expert witness. *Hospital and Community Psychiatry, 44,* 388–389.

Sleek, S. (1995). Walker defends rights to testify for O. J. *The APA Monitor, 26*(4), 8.

Smith, V. P. (Ed.). (1997). *Algebraic K-theory*. Providence, RI: American Mathematical Society.

Walker, L. E. (1979). *The battered woman*. New York: Harper & Row.

Walker, L. E. (1989). *Terrifying love: Why battered women kill and how society responds*. New York: Harper & Row.

Watzlawick, P. (1983). *The situation is hopeless, but not serious: The pursuit of unhappiness*. New York: Norton.

Ziskin, J., & Faust, D. (1988). *Coping with psychiatric and psychological testimony* (4th ed., Vols. 1–3). Los Angeles, CA: Law and Psychology Press.

Ziskin, J. (1995). *Coping with psychiatric and psychological testimony* (5th ed., Vols. 1–3). Los Angeles, CA: Law and Psychology Press.

Appendix: Recommended Readings

Ceci, S. J., & Hembrooke, H. (Eds.). (1998). *Expert witnesses in child abuse cases: What can and should be said in court.* Washington, DC: American Psychological Association.

Although the thirteen chapters in this book reach too broadly, from roles of experts in the common law all the way to validity of child sexual abuse validations, this book stands out as the best of the flurry of recent books on testifying in child sexual abuse cases. Maggie Bruck's chapter on her experiences in court is wonderfully illuminating. The contributors are a "Who's Who" on expert testimony and child abuse expertise. But I wish Steve Ceci had contributed his own incisive views.

Feder, H. A. (1991). *Succeeding as an expert witness: Increasing your impact and income.* Glenwood Springs, CO: Tageh Press.

This book describes the interesting results of a survey of 54 testifying experts who responded to a survey mailed to 160 experts. This book skims lightly where deeper examination of content and issues is warranted.

Gutheil, T. G. (1998). *The psychiatrist as expert witness.* Washington, DC: American Psychiatric Press.

This is a terrific book. I was delighted and charmed by the way the book ranges through the whole practice of forensic evaluations, from ethics to evaluation methods and testimony to writing reports and marketing a practice. Gutheil has a nifty way with a phrase and discusses fascinating cases. Let me note that one chapter, about the expert on the road, I found irrelevant. It was apparently written for experts who have never been on airplanes, and advises purchasing a good carry-on suitcase, a lined toiletry kit, and to be certain to seek out frequent flier benefits. Really!

Jenkins, P. J., & Kroll-Smith, S. (Eds.). (1996). *Witnessing for sociology: Sociologists in court.* Westport, CT: Praeger.

Who knew that sociologists testify on at least as many topics as do psychologists? Certainly not my sociologist partner! In his afterword, Kai Erikson observed,

> So, our biggest problem, frequently, is to find ways to describe things that seem wholly self-evident to those of us who share a sociological way of looking at the human world. It can be hard. However, I often am amazed at how receptive judges and lawyers and, especially, juries can be to the oblique wisdoms we bring to court. (p. 250)

A fine book.

Lubet, S. (1998). *Expert testimony: A guide to expert witnesses and the lawyers who examine them.* Notre Dame, IN: National Institute for Trial Advocacy.

The author achieves three objectives in this book. First, he seemlessly integrates legal standards affecting expert witnesses into the general text. Second, he translates psychological principles relating to witness credibility and testimony in discussions so that they are more accessible and meaningful than in any writings I have seen by psychologists. Third, he writes with a remarkable clarity that should be the envy of other authors of professional books.

Matson, J. V. (1990). *Effective expert witnessing: A handbook for technical professionals.* Chelsea, MI: Lewis.

Jack Matson specializes in cross-examination questions in this book written especially for engineers, chemists, and other technical specialties. However, the principles apply to many other expert witnesses, and are thoughtful and well-developed. Almost one third of the 125 pages of text in the book is devoted to a chapter titled

"The engineer's nightmare: A case study." Much of this chapter is out of step with the rest of the book and not useful.

Shuy, R. W. (1993). *Language crimes: The use and abuse of language evidence in the courtroom*. Cambridge, MA: Blackwell.

The author writes mostly about analyses of language and meaning in cases of alleged bribery, threats, agreements, and so on. Although the content is modestly useful as background for appreciating language use, the content is targeted toward linguists and lawyers and is less helpful for other experts.

Stern, P. (1997). *Preparing and presenting expert testimony in child abuse litigation: A guide for expert witnesses and attorneys*. Thousand Oaks, CA: Sage.

Stern aimed this book at both attorneys and expert witnesses, but reaches neither. In the expert testimony section, a contributed chapter by social worker Benjamin Saunders is exceptionally useful in a book that overall does not deliver enough substance about preparation for child abuse testimony.

Tsushima, W. T., & Anderson, R. M., Jr. (1996). *Mastering expert testimony: A courtroom handbook for mental health professionals*. Mahwah, NJ: Erlbaum.

Thorough, thoughtful, and comprehensive, this book provides an excellent examination of common questions and problems faced by mental health professionals on the witness stand. The suggestions are based on the presentation of typical questions asked of psychological expert witnesses, and responses that are more masterful and less masterful are presented. The Tsushima and Anderson book is an excellent choice.

About the Author

Stanley L. Brodsky is Professor of Psychology at the University of Alabama, where he coordinates the Psychology–Law PhD concentration. He is the author of 10 books and 160 articles and chapters, mostly in psychology applied to legal issues. Among other honors, he was the 1996 recipient of the Distinguished Contribution Award for Outstanding Achievement in Forensic Psychology by the American Academy of Forensic Psychology. His book *Testifying in Court: Guidelines and Maxims for the Expert Witness*, published in 1991 by the American Psychological Association, has become a major source book for expert witnesses. He maintains an independent practice in forensic psychology and he is a frequent leader of workshops on court testimony and forensic psychology.